"Jesus, Wondrous Saviour"

The roots and legacy of some Ontario Baptists, 1810s–1920s

These illuminating accounts of notable British and Ontario Baptist movements and leaders are essential reading for anyone interested in the history of those who shaped Baptist identity in our country. Focusing primarily on theological perspectives, education and controversies, these Ontario vignettes bring to light many of the roots, struggles and successes that informed the Canadian Baptist experience. Once again, Michael Haykin's diligent research and thoughtful presentation of his work has expanded and deepened our understanding of the many valuable but often overlooked contributions that Baptists from Ontario made to this country.

Paul R. Wilson, *President of the Canadian Baptist Historical Society*

If anyone should wonder about the Baptist heritage in Ontario, they should read Michael Haykin's *"Jesus, wondrous Saviour": The roots and legacy of some Ontario Baptists, 1810s–1920s*. Haykin's gift for narration is sure to whet the appetite of casual readers and scholars alike. Graceful. Edifying. Highly recommended.

Keith Harper, *Southeastern Baptist Theological Seminary*

Michael Haykin's affectionate, yet unvarnished, history of Baptists in Ontario weaves the lives of individual leaders with that of the development of a regional movement. It is an account of endurance through many hardships, setbacks and, sometimes, conflict, but it is, above all, the story of God's faithfulness to his people.

David Luke, *Tutor in Historical Theology and Church History, Irish Baptist College*

In short, readable, and well-documented chapters, Michael Haykin examines from a conservative perspective the stories of key men, institutions, and controversies that shaped Ontario Baptists. Baptists in Canada and beyond are indebted to Haykin for this insightful history of Ontario Baptists in the long nineteenth century.

Melody Maxwell, *Associate Professor of Christian History, Acadia Divinity College*

As Dr Haykin states in this volume, the Baptist world has a robust and rich history. As far as Canada is concerned that rich history is under explored. This volume focuses on a small part of it – the story of the Ontario Baptist community from its origins up to the 1920s. It whets the appetite for more and will be of interest not only to Canadian Baptists but to all who love the work of the Lord and want to know more about it. Not uncritical in its appraisal, the book seeks to remind us of a small but significant part of the work of the wondrous Saviour in history.

Gary Brady, *Pastor of Childs Hill Baptist Church, London, UK*

In "Jesus, Wondrous Savior," Dr. Haykin writes about key figures used by God to advance the cause of the gospel in Canada whose lives and ministries shape our own. His fascinating account is a timely reminder of the great debt we owe to those who have gone before and that our struggles are not only similar but part of a divine plan and never in vain.

Kirk Wellum, *Principal, Toronto Baptist Seminary*

In Psalm 107:43 (NLT) it states: *Those who are wise will take all this to heart; they will see in our history the faithful love of the Lord.* Knowing at least a little about our past is required to make sense of the present and plan for the future. Ontario Baptists, through this study of aspects of their story, can gain a window into the lives of some key Baptist leaders that have contributed to their witness since the early nineteenth century. I hope this well-written study stimulates its readers to explore further the Ontario Baptist heritage. It is warmly commended.

Dr Brian R. Talbot, *Minister Broughty Ferry Baptist Church, Dundee, & Dept of Theology, North-West University, South Africa*

"Jesus, Wondrous Saviour"

The roots and legacy of some Ontario Baptists, 1810s–1920s

Americus Vespucius Timpany (1840-1885) and his wife Jane Bates Timpany went to India as Ontario's first Baptist missionaries.

"Jesus, Wondrous Saviour"
The roots and legacy of some Ontario Baptists, 1810s–1920s

Michael A. G. Haykin

ALEV Books
168 Cornwallis Road
Ancaster, ON
Canada L9C 4H3
www.alevbooks.com

ISBN: 978-1-7752353-3-0

Layout by ALEVBooks
Cover by Janice Van Eck

Keywords: Baptist, Ontario, 19th century theological education, R.A. Fyfe, McMaster University, communion.

Copyright © 2023, Michael A.G. Haykin
Author's webpage: www.andrewfullercenter.org

All rights reserved. No part of this publication may be reproduced or transmitted in any form or by any means, graphic, electronic, or mechanical, including photocopying, recording, or any information storage and retrieval system without permission in writing from the copyright holder.

To Graham and Nancy Lowe
For their many kindnesses and love

Contents

♦ ♦ ♦

Foreword, Prof. Gordon Heath	3
Introduction: On becoming a Baptist in Ontario	5
Acknowledgements	9
1. Our Scottish Baptist Roots	11
2. William Fraser & the Breadalbane Baptists	19
3. Baptist Polemics	31
4. Canada Baptist College & Benjamin Davies	41
5. Robert Alexander Fyfe & the Canadian Literary Institute	51
6. John Harvard Castle & William McMaster	59
7. Jarvis Street Baptist Church & Toronto Baptist College	67
8. A Welsh Baptist: Benjamin Daniel Thomas	75
9. "Dr. Thomas of Toronto"	83
10. Daniel Arthur McGregor & "The McMaster Hymn"	91
11. T.T. Shields & the Importance of learning	105
Appendix 1: Benjamin Davies, "The Importance of Education for Those who Undertake the Work of the Ministry"	119
Appendix 2: The Statement of Faith in the Toronto Baptist College Act of Incorporation	131
Appendix 3: "Worship at Jarvis Street Baptist Church"—a newspaper account from April, 1895	133

Foreword

♦ ♦ ♦

Lawrence S. Cunningham writes, "Lives of the saints were part and parcel of the spiritual formation of serious Christians from the time of antiquity."[1] While the Baptists in this volume would not have called themselves "saints" in the sense being referred to by Cunningham, the point still stands. Those who are serious about being informed and inspired in the faith should read of the lives of those who have lived godly lives and carried out heroic deeds often in the face of harsh circumstances. And that is what makes this book good reading.

Baptists in Canada have a rich but often unexplored history. Consequently, Michael Haykin has done a great service by exploring figures—whether unknown, well-known, loved, or not loved—who have shaped the history of Ontario Baptists.

The period covered in this volume often included harsh frontier conditions, lack of church resources, nascent organizations, restricted communications, limited educational opportunities, and, for many, a vast distance from their European families. Along with those challenges went weekly pastoral care and preparation for services. Yet, in the midst of those challenges, Baptists, led by such figures as explored in this book, toiled away to build the church into the early years of the twentieth century.

Of course, that does not mean that every decision made by those leaders was right or wise, or every leader perfect. (Even my friend Michael and I differ in our interpretations in some areas.) But there is a telling of the story here that informs our sense of the past and deepens our awareness of the heritage of Christianity in Canada in general, and Baptists in Ontario in particular. And that is (or should be) the interest of "serious Christians."

Prof. Gordon Heath

---

[1] Lawrence S. Cunningham, *A Brief History of Saints* (Malden: Blackwell, 2005), 136.

The interior of Stanley Avenue Baptist Church, circa 1925

Introduction: On Becoming a Baptist in Ontario

◆ ◆ ◆

WHEN I WAS converted in February of 1974, I was attending Stanley Avenue Baptist Church in Hamilton, Ontario, which belonged to the Fellowship of Evangelical Baptist Churches in Canada. I had been raised in the environment of pre-Vatican II Roman Catholicism and initially Baptist worship seemed to me quite *outré*. However, even more troubling to me was the fact that, shortly after my conversion, I asked a deacon of the church to give me a historical overview of where Baptists came from (I cannot remember a time when I have not loved history). But he really had no idea. This ignorance about the history of the people called Baptists troubled me deeply for much of the 1970s and very early 1980s. What was the historical identity of this community that I had joined?

It was not until I was asked to teach Baptist history at Central Baptist Seminary around 1983, where I had become a professor of church history the year before, that I became aware of the robust and rich history of the Baptist world. That discovery eventually led to a focus in my academic research on the British and Irish Baptist world of the eighteenth century. And given my domicile in Ontario, it is not surprising that I have also been involved over the years in tracing and researching the experience of the Ontario Baptist community. The book that you hold in your hands is partially the fruit of that research.

At the close of the 1990s, conversations with the late William H. Brackney (1948–2022) initially gave me the idea of a history of the Ontario Baptists. Further discussions with three Canadian church historians—Donald Goertz, Mark Steinacher, and Paul Wilson—around 2000 deepened my conviction that a history of Baptists in the province of Ontario was greatly needed. This volume is by no means the full story of the Ontario Baptist community from its origins in the wake of the American Revolution to the 1920s. That would require a much more extensive tome. Nonetheless, these chapters do highlight a number of key figures from this era as well as some central themes, especially those of theological education, doctrinal controversy and the search for unity, and confessional orthodoxy and piety.

Undergirding this study of the Ontario Baptist world in what one can call the long nineteenth century is the conviction that by the 1890s there was a broad theological consensus among the Baptists of Ontario and that this was summarized in the statement of faith in the trust deed of Toronto Baptist College (see Appendix 2).[2] In fine, this consensus can be described as one that was confessionally Calvinistic, unashamedly Baptistic, and committed to closed communion. At the very same time, however, there were theological forces at work that eventually tore this unity apart forty or so years later in the 1920s. And while that controversy did at times get bogged down in issues of power and matters of personality, at its heart was the recognition by a goodly number of Baptists in Ontario that McMaster University was departing from some of its theological moorings.[3] In an incisive reflection on the course of this controversy, the late George A. Rawlyk (1935–1996) briefly imagined a counter-factual history of the McMaster controversy in which McMaster stayed true to its roots and became "a small, reputable Christian college."[4] That, of course, was not the pathway of history. And yet, in the closing decades of the twentieth century, through the leadership of the late William Brackney, the Divinity College at McMaster University did return to its roots, which form the heart of the story told in this book. And for that renewal, which has been ongoing under the presidency and deanship of Dr. Stan Porter, I for one am deeply thankful.

---

[2] See, in this regard, William Gillespie, "The Recovery of Ontario's Baptist Tradition" in *Memory and Hope: Strands of Canadian Baptist History*, ed. David T. Priestley (Waterloo, ON: Wilfrid Laurier University Press for the Canadian Corporation for Studies in Religion/Corporation Canadienne des Sciences Religieuses, 1996), 25–37.

[3] Colin R. Godwin, "Ignorant Fundamentalists? Ministerial Education as a factor in the Fundamentalist/Modernist Controversy in the Baptist Convention of Ontario and Quebec, 1927–1933," *Pacific Journal of Baptist Research* 4, no.1 (April 2008): 15.

[4] George A. Rawlyk, *Canadian Baptists and Christian Higher Education* (Kingston, ON; Montreal, QC: McGill-Queen's University Press, 1988), 121–122, n.87.

The various chapters in this book originated in different contexts, which I have delineated below.

Chapters 1–3 originally appeared as "Voluntarism in the Life and Ministry of William Fraser (1801–1883)" in William H. Brackney, ed., *The Believers Church: A Voluntary Church. Papers of the Twelfth Believers Church Conference held at McMaster Divinity College, October 17–19, 1996* (Kitchener, ON: Pandora Press, 1998), 25–50. Used by kind permission.

Chapter 4 originally appeared as "'We desire a learned ministry…we desire a pious ministry': Remembering the vision of Benjamin Davies for Canada Baptist College" in *For Christ and His Church: Essays in service of the church and its mission* (Kitchener, ON; Joshua Press, 2015), 9–16. Used by kind permission.

Chapters 6–7 originally appeared in Michael A.G. Haykin and Roy M. Paul, *Set for the Defense of the Gospel: A Bicentennial History of Jarvis Street Baptist Church, 1818–2018* (Toronto, ON: Jarvis Street Baptist Church, 2018). Used by permission.

Most of Chapters 8–9 first appeared as "Dr. Thomas of Toronto: The Life and Ministry of Benjamin Daniel Thomas (1843–1917)," *The Gospel Witness* 87, no.1 (June 2008): 7–12. They were also published in Michael A.G. Haykin and Roy M. Paul, *Set for the Defense of the Gospel: A Bicentennial History of Jarvis Street Baptist Church, 1818–2018* (Toronto, ON: Jarvis Street Baptist Church, 2018). Used by kind permission.

The bulk of Chapter 10 appears in Dave Barker and Michael A.G. Haykin, ed., *Life is Worship: A Festschrift in Honour of Douglas A. Thomson on the occasion of his Seventieth Birthday* (Cambridge, ON: Heritage Seminary Press, 2023). Used by kind permission.

Acknowledgments

For help with the research that went into the various chapters of this book, I would especially like to thank Prof. Donald Meek, one-time Professor of Celtic at the University of Aberdeen; Paul DeGraaf, a one-time pastor of Breadalbane Baptist Church, Dalkeith, ON; Judith Colwell and Adam McCulloch, a former and current Archivist at the Canadian Baptist Archives, McMaster Divinity College, Hamilton, ON; Vicky Cooper, Registrar of the Bruce County Museum and Archives, Southampton, ON; the late George Thomas, pastor of Tiverton Baptist Church, Tiverton, ON; the staff of the Owen Sound Public Library; David S.G. and Debbie Livingston-Lowe, my brother- and sister-in-law, who were extremely helpful with regard to "things Gaelic"; the late Revd. and Mrs. Graham Harrison of Newport, Wales; and Revd. and Mrs. Chris Rees of Narberth, Pembrokeshire, Wales; Jordan A. Senécal, the present librarian of Heritage Theological Seminary in Cambridge, ON; my daughter Victoria Haykin, who was my research assistant during the summer of 2008; Caleb Neel for his transcription of Appendix 3; Pastor Daniel Morden of Jarvis Street Baptist Church, Toronto; and Dr. Roy Paul, my present research assistant at the Canadian office of the Andrew Fuller Centre for Baptist Studies.

JAMES ALEXANDER HALDANE

1
Our Scottish Baptist Roots

♦ ♦ ♦

WHILE BAPTIST CONGREGATIONS could be found in most parts of England and Wales by the beginning of the eighteenth century, there were virtually none in Scotland until the last few decades of this era. The national church which was Presbyterian had become so fused with what it meant to be Scottish that Baptist principles seemed completely alien to the Scottish mind. Extremely influential in this regard was the first theological standard of Scottish Presbyterianism, the *Scots Confession*. Drawn up in 1560 by John Knox (*c.*1513–1572) and five other Reformed ministers, this text was adamant in its opposition to believer's baptism: "we damn the error of the Anabaptists, who denies baptism to appertain to children, before that they have faith and understanding."[5]

The first noteworthy appearance of Baptist communities on Scottish soil was in the brief period of time between the defeat of the Scots by Oliver Cromwell's New Model Army at the Battle of Dunbar on September 3, 1650, and the death of Cromwell eight years later. A goodly number of Cromwell's army officers were Baptist in their convictions, and they wasted no time in establishing congregations in the towns where they were garrisoned. Cromwell himself had sought to convince the Scottish Presbyterians of the rightness of tolerating expressions of biblical Christianity other than their own. "Is all religion wrapped up in that or any one form?," he asked the Scots in a public

---

[5] *Confessio Fidei Scoticana* XXIII in Philip Schaff, ed. and David S. Schaff, revised, *The Creeds of Christendom* (1931, Grand Rapids, MI: Baker Book House, 1983), III, 474. This sentence has been modernized. My attention was drawn to this text by its inclusion in D.B. Murray, "The Seventeenth and Eighteenth Centuries" in D. W. Bebbington, ed., *The Baptists in Scotland. A History* (Glasgow: The Baptist Union of Scotland, 1988), 9–25, an article that is extremely helpful in tracing Baptist history in Scotland prior to 1800.

declaration in 1650. "We think not so. We say, faith working by love is the true character of a Christian; and, God is our witness, in whomsoever we see any thing of Christ to be, there we reckon our duty to love."[6] Scottish Presbyterians, though, remained unconvinced and the restoration of Charles II to the throne in 1660 extinguished all of these Cromwellian expressions of the Baptist faith.

Close to a century was to pass before a Baptist congregation was once again found in Scotland. It was in 1765 that the so-called Scotch Baptists, also known as the McLeanite Baptists after their chief theologian and apologist, Archibald McLean (1733–1812), came into existence.[7] About thirty years later, in the mid-1790s, two wealthy brothers James Haldane (1768–1851) and his older brother Robert (1764–1842), experienced what we would call a conversion to evangelical Christianity.[8] Within a few years of their conversion both

---

[6] Oliver Cromwell, *A Declaration of the Army of England upon their March into Scotland To all that are Saints, and Partakers of the Faith of God's Elect, in Scotland* in Wilbur Cortez Abbott, *The Writings and Speeches of Oliver Cromwell* (Cambridge, MA: Harvard University Press, 1939), II, 285–286. During the second phase of the Civil War, which lasted from 1648 to 1651, the Scots, who had fought with the parliamentary armies during the first phase of the war from 1642 to 1646, took the side of the Stuart monarchy. Cromwell and his army invaded Scotland in July 1650. This passage is from a much longer text that seeks to convince the Scots that they and the English share a common Reformed heritage, and that therefore they should not be meeting as enemies on the battlefield.

[7] On the Scotch Baptists, see Murray, "Seventeenth and Eighteenth Centuries," 19–24.

[8] The standard life of the Haldanes is that of James' son, Alexander Haldane, *The Lives of Robert and James Haldane* (1852, Edinburgh: The Banner of Truth Trust, 1990). For more recent studies, see D.B. Murray and D.E. Meek, "The Early Nineteenth Century" in Bebbington, ed., *Baptists in Scotland*, 30–32; Deryck W. Lovegrove, "Unity and Separation: Contrasting Elements in the Thought and Practice of Robert and James Alexander Haldane" in Keith Robbins, ed., *Protestant Evangelicalism: Britain, Ireland, Germany and America c.1750–c.1950. Essays in Honour of W. R. Ward* (Oxford: Basil Blackwell, 1990), 153–177; Kenneth J. Stewart, "Restoring the Reformation: British Evangelicalism and the 'Reveil' at Geneva 1816–1849" (PhD thesis, University of Edinburgh, 1991), 59–66, 126–169; Deryck Lovegrove, "Haldane, James Alexander" in Donald M. Lewis, ed., *The Blackwell Dictionary of Evangelical Biography 1730–1860* (Oxford; Cambridge, MA: Blackwell Publishers Ltd., 1995), I, 501; Kenneth J. Stewart, "Haldane, Robert" in Lewis, ed., *Blackwell Dictionary of Evangelical Biography*, I, 501–502.

of the Haldane brothers were undertaking extensive preaching tours of the Highlands and the Orkneys, where their preaching often drew large crowds. In 1797 the brothers founded the Society for the Propagation of the Gospel at Home (SPGH), the first Protestant society concerned with spreading Protestant Christianity throughout the Highlands, and Robert used his considerable wealth to finance the promotion of this venture. Robert's generosity was displayed in the support of the Society's itinerant preachers, the publication of religious tracts and bibles, the purchase and building of Congregationalist worship centres, and the creation of a theological seminary, which trained nearly three hundred students in the nine years of its existence from 1799 to 1808. It has been estimated that Robert spent some £70,000 in home missionary ventures related to this Society between 1798 and 1810.[9] Central to its *raison d'être* was the non-denominational character of the organization. "It is not our design to form or to extend the influence of any sect," the founders declared. "Our sole intention is to make known the everlasting gospel of our Lord Jesus Christ." Those who ministered under its auspices were thus expected to "discourage all bitter party spirit, wherever they discover it."[10]

In 1808, however, the Haldanes aroused considerable controversy in the churches that they had planted and financed when they embraced the Baptist conviction of believer's baptism by immersion. Not surprisingly, their advocacy of believer's baptism brought about the collapse of the SPGH. At the same time, though, their embrace of Baptist views was a major stimulus to the Scottish Baptist movement. Of the forty-one Baptist churches in existence in Scotland by 1810, twenty-three of them had their origins between 1808 and 1810, and

---

[9] R.F. Calder, "Robert Haldane's Theological Seminary," *Transactions of the Congregational Historical Society* 13 (1937–1939): 59–63, 53; D.W. Lovegrove, "Haldane, Robert" in Nigel M. De S. Cameron, David F. Wright, David C. Lachman, and Donald E. Meek, ed., *Dictionary of Scottish Church History & Theology* (Downers Grove, IL: InterVarsity Press, 1993), 386.
[10] Cited Lovegrove, "Unity and Separation" in Robbins, ed., *Protestant Evangelicalism*, 155.

most of these were linked to the controversy surrounding the Haldanes' move from Congregationalism to Baptist convictions.[11]

Now, a number of these Baptist causes were Gaelic-speaking congregations in the Highlands, or the Gàidhealtachd, where Gaelic was the mother tongue. The Presbyterian Church in the Lowlands, where English and Scots—the latter, like English, a derivative from Old English—were primarily spoken, had been convinced for much of the seventeenth and eighteenth centuries that "true" religion and "civilized" behaviour could only be inculcated through the medium of English and Anglo-Scottish culture.[12] Although some provision was made for ministry in Gaelic and there were a few attempts in the seventeenth century to publish a full translation of the Scriptures in Gaelic, it is not without significance that a Gaelic New Testament did not appear until 1767 and a complete Bible until 1801.[13] The appearance of this translation, however, was linked to a growing realization among Scottish Lowland Evangelicals that Gaelic was critical for the evangelization of the Highlands. Various missionary efforts in cross-cultural contexts, in particular that of English Baptists in India, had inspired Scottish Lowland Evangelicals like the Haldanes to reflect on the mission field immediately to their north.[14] Moreover,

---

[11] Murray and Meek, "Early Nineteenth Century," 32; D.E. Meek, "The Highlands" in Bebbington, ed., *Baptists in Scotland*, 284–285. On this controversy, see D.E. Meek, "The Independent and Baptist Churches of Highland Perthshire and Strathspey," *Transactions of the Gaelic Society of Inverness* 56 (1988–1990): 281–287.

[12] Victor Edward Durkacz, *The Decline of the Celtic Languages. A Study of Linguistic and Cultural Conflict in Scotland, Wales and Ireland from the Reformation to the Twentieth Century* (Edinburgh: John Donald Publishers Ltd., 1983), 9–14; Jane Dawson, "Calvinism and the Gaidhealtachd in Scotland" in Andrew Pettegree, Alastair Duke and Gillian Lewis, *Calvinism in Europe, 1540–1620* (Cambridge: Cambridge University Press, 1994), 252. See also the remarks of Donald E. Meek, "Language and Style in the Scottish Gaelic Bible (1767–1807)," *Scottish Language* 9 (Winter, 1990): 1.

[13] For this Bible, see especially Donald E. Meek, "Bible (Versions, Gaelic)" in De S. Cameron, Wright, Lachman, and Meek, ed., *Dictionary of Scottish Church History & Theology*, 75–76.

[14] On the broad impact of Carey and his colleagues, see William H. Brackney, *Christian Voluntarism in Britain and North America: A Bibliography and Critical Assessment* (Westport, CT; London: Greenwood Press, 1995), 43–45.

OUR SCOTTISH BAPTIST ROOTS

Scottish Evangelicals who became involved in the evangelization of the Highlands from the 1790s onward were increasingly conscious of the importance of Gaelic for the accomplishment of this task.

Of the various Gaelic-speaking Baptist congregations in the Highlands, "the largest and most productive" was that at Grantown-on-Spey, Morayshire.[15] In fact, one of the factors said to have induced James Haldane to submit to believer's baptism was the example set by the pastor of this church, Lachlan Mackintosh (d.1857), who had been converted under James Haldane's preaching in 1803.[16] Mackintosh publicly announced his commitment to Baptist views in 1807 and was baptized the following year. With the backing of his congregation, the Grantown-on-Spey church was then re-organized as a Baptist work and in time became, in the words of Donald Meek, a "nursery of powerful Baptist preachers."[17] A central reason for the impact of the Grantown church was undoubtedly the man who succeeded Mackintosh as pastor in 1826, Peter Grant (1783–1867), who had been converted through the preaching of his predecessor.[18] Grant, whose pastorate lasted till his death in 1867, was the possessor of considerable evangelistic, teaching and hymn-writing gifts. In fact, he is one of Scotland's best-known composers of Gaelic hymns, hymns that are still well-known in all the Protestant denominations in the Highlands.

Under Grant's ministry the church became the centre of an extremely vigorous movement of evangelism and outreach in the Strathspey valley and far beyond. Here, fledgling Baptist preachers

---

[15] Donald E. Meek, "Mackintosh, Lachlan" in Lewis, ed., *Blackwell Dictionary of Evangelical Biography*, II, 725.

[16] For Mackintosh, see Meek, "Independent and Baptist Churches," 282; *idem*, "Mackintosh, Lachlan" in Lewis, ed., *Blackwell Dictionary of Evangelical Biography*, II, 725–726

[17] Meek, "Independent and Baptist Churches," 287.

[18] For Grant, see Donald E. Meek, "Grant, Peter" in Lewis, ed., *Blackwell Dictionary of Evangelical Biography*, I, 467, and his unpublished paper, " 'The Glory of the Lamb': The Gaelic Hymnody of Peter Grant" (The First International Conference on Baptist Studies, Regent's Park College, Oxford, August, 1997); Terry L. Wilder, ed., *The Lost Sermons of Scottish Baptist Peter Grant, the Highland Herald* (Mountain Home, AR; Memphis, TN; Dallas, TX: BorderStone Press, 2010); George J. Mitchell, *Highland Harvester—Peter Grant's Life, Times and Legacy* (n.p., 2013).

were nurtured in a vigorous evangelical Christianity, which, yoked to a deep commitment to believer's baptism, enabled them to challenge the established Presbyterianism of the Highlands.[19] In certain districts of the Highlands, notably the north-west, "the Men" (*na Daoine*), a "spiritual élite who acted as the custodians and leaders of experiential religion" of Highland Presbyterianism, were powerful enough to prevent Baptist congregations taking root.[20] In other areas, though, particularly Perthshire and the Inner Hebrides, Baptist congregations were planted which flourished and which would in time provide men and women who would be in the forefront of the Baptist movement in Canada. One such Baptist, William Fraser, is the main subject of our next chapter.

---

[19] Meek, "Independent and Baptist Churches," 287.
[20] Meek, "Highlands," 287. On "the Men," see D. E. Meek, "Men, The" in De S. Cameron, Wright, Lachman, and Meek, ed., *Dictionary of Scottish Church History & Theology*, 558–559.

A drawing of Breadalbane in the 1830s

2

William Fraser and the Breadalbane Baptists

♦ ♦ ♦

Early Years in Scotland, 1801–1831

BORN IN 1801 into a farming family, William Fraser (1801–1883) was raised among the rugged and imposing scenery of Strathspey.[21] His parents belonged to the Church of Scotland, but theirs was a nominal Christianity. So Fraser grew up regarding himself as a Christian, completely unaware of the fact that he needed to experience conversion. Around the age of sixteen, though, a number of Scripture passages awakened him to the true nature of his spiritual condition. Not long after, he heard Peter Grant preach and, in the words of the Irish-Canadian Baptist John Dempsey, he was "enabled to receive the Lord Jesus as his own Saviour."[22] Soon after his conversion Grant spoke to him about his need to declare his faith publicly in believer's baptism. Having been raised in the Church of Scotland, Fraser wrestled with this request for some time. Eventually, though, he came to the conviction that this was the only baptism known by the New Testament church, a conviction from which he never wavered. He was

---

[21] For the following details of Fraser's life, I am indebted to John Dempsey, "The Late Rev. W. Fraser," *The Canadian Baptist* 28, no. 38 (October 4, 1883): 8; idem, "William Fraser," *The McMaster University Monthly* 8 (1898–1899): 241–248; Donald E. Meek, "Evangelicalism and Emigration: Aspects of the Role of Dissenting Evangelicalism in Highland Emigration to Canada" in Gordon W. MacLennan, ed., *Proceedings of the First North American Congress of Celtic Studies* (Ottawa, ON: Chair of Celtic Studies, University of Ottawa, 1988), 27–31; idem, "Fraser, William" in Nigel M. De S. Cameron, David F. Wright, David C. Lachman, and Donald E. Meek, ed., *Dictionary of Scottish Church History & Theology* (Downers Grove, IL: InterVarsity Press, 1993), 336.
[22] Dempsey, "William Fraser," 243.

baptized by his pastor, Lachlan Mackintosh, and joined the Grantown-on-Spey church.

From 1823 to 1825 Fraser studied at the Haldane seminary in Grantown-on-Spey under Mackintosh's supervision.[23] Having completed his studies, he served as an itinerant preacher for a year in the Highlands and adjacent regions of the Lowlands. Trekking over the wildest of hillsides in all types of weather would have built up reserves of physical fortitude and stamina, which would serve him in good stead later during his pastorate in the Ottawa Valley. Fraser's ministry during this year would have consisted of two circuits. The "home circuit" would be covered during the winter months, while the longer circuit, undertaken during the summer, might well take over two months to cover.[24] Having to preach often in the open air would also have developed Fraser's skills as a communicator and Baptist apologist.[25] On more than one occasion as he spoke Fraser probably would have had to deal with local authorities or "the Men." Christopher Anderson (1782–1852), pastor of the Baptist cause in Richmond Court, Edinburgh, and one of William Carey's most faithful British supporters, describes in his diary an encounter with local authorities that was not at all atypical. In 1805 he was present at the formation of Bellanoch Baptist Church, Argyllshire, whose first pastor was Donald McVicar (fl.1800–1820), who had studied under the Haldanes and who later emigrated to Canada in the 1810s.[26] The day following the actual constitution of the church an open-air baptismal service was being held when the factor of the Bellanoch landlord, Malcolm of Poltalloch, appeared on the scene and, in the words of Anderson, "said he had a general order to stop all such preaching on

---

[23] Dempsey wrongly states that this seminary was in Edinburgh ("William Fraser," 243). On the seminary in Grantown-on-Spey, see also Alexander Haldane, *The Lives of Robert and James Haldane* (1852, Edinburgh: The Banner of Truth Trust, 1990), 331.

[24] Haldane, *The Lives of Robert and James Haldane*, 288.

[25] D.E. Meek, "The Independent and Baptist Churches of Highland Perthshire and Strathspey," *Transactions of the Gaelic Society of Inverness* 56 (1988–1990): 276, 287.

[26] On McVicar, see Donald E. Meek, "McVicar, Donald" in Lewis, ed., *Blackwell Dictionary of Evangelical Biography*, II, 733.

the estate, and would call out the Volunteers if we did nor desist!"[27] And we know of at least one occasion when Fraser, preaching on the isle of Lewis, "spent four hours of a Sabbath day discussing on the inability and sinfulness of infant baptism." We owe this reference to one of the more liberal ministers on the island, John Cameron, who further referred to Fraser and other like-minded Baptists as a "swarm of dissenters who came to Lewis to pounce upon the poor people, like common carrion."[28]

In 1826 Fraser was asked to oversee the Baptist work in Uig on the Isle of Skye. This church had come into existence around 1808.[29] Four years later a chapel, capable of accommodating three hundred people, was built beside the River Conon, where outdoor baptisms were held. During Fraser's first year of ministry the membership of the church grew to around sixty, and it was said that a "considerable number," as many as three hundred, attended the worship services of the church. The large difference between members and adherents/"listeners" was typical of most of Highland Baptist churches during this period. As Donald Meek has observed, "the level of adherency for a single church would have ranged from five to ten times the size of the membership."[30] A number of these Baptist churches, moreover, appear to have had difficulty retaining adherents/"listeners" over the long run. In part this was due to the fact that the voluntarism of their church life clashed with the nature of Highland society which was strongly based on extended family networks. The latter was better suited to Presbyterianism.[31]

On July 27, 1828, Fraser was "set apart to the pastoral office by prayer, with fasting" in the presence of his congregation and a number of pastors. One of the pastors, Dugald Sinclair (1777–1870), an itinerant preacher who prepared the soil for the emergence of a

---

[27] Hugh Anderson, *The Life and Letters of Christopher Anderson* (Edinburgh: William P. Kennedy, 1854), 26–27.
[28] Cited Meek, "Independent and Baptist Churches," 289.
[29] For the early history of this church, I am indebted to Meek, "Independent and Baptist Churches," 333–339.
[30] Meek, "Independent and Baptist Churches," 293.
[31] Meek, "Independent and Baptist Churches," 293–294.

number of Gaelic-speaking Calvinistic Baptist churches in the Inner Hebrides, gave the charge to Fraser from Acts 20:28 ("Take heed therefore unto yourselves, and to all the flock, over the which the Holy Ghost hath made you overseers, to feed the church of God, which he hath purchased with his own blood" [KJV]).[32] Over the next four years, however, a goodly number of the church members emigrated and by 1831 church membership was down to twenty-three.

Between the last quarter of the eighteenth century and 1870 various waves of emigration swept over the Gaelic-speaking Highlands which transplanted entire communities of Highlanders to the American continent. It has been estimated that during this period some 185,000 Scots left their homeland for Canada.[33] Reasons for emigrating were various. In the late eighteenth century many went to Canada in order to escape the winds of change that were sweeping over the Highlands and thus preserve their pastoral way of life. Traditional methods of farming were being phased out, home-based industries were losing ground in the face of industrialization, and the clan chiefs were turning the people off the land so as to make way for more lucrative sheep-farms or deer-forests.[34] In addition, the years following the British victory over the French in the Napoleonic Wars saw general economic depression throughout Great Britain. The kelping industry, which was a main source of livelihood in many areas of the Inner and Outer Hebrides, virtually collapsed overnight, and many were driven overseas out of economic necessity. Fraser himself decided to emigrate

---

[32] *Report of the Baptist Home Missionary Society for Scotland, chiefly for the Highlands and Islands*, (1829): 33–36; Donald E. Meek, "Evangelicalism and Emigration: Aspects of the Role of Dissenting Evangelicalism in Highland Emigration to Canada" in Gordon W. MacLennan, ed., *Proceedings of the First North American Congress of Celtic Studies* (Ottawa, ON: Chair of Celtic Studies, University of Ottawa, 1988), 30. Sinclair emigrated to Ontario in 1831, where he assumed the pastoral leadership of what would eventually become Poplar Hill Christian Church, Ilderton. For Sinclair, see especially Donald E. Meek, "Dugald Sinclair: The Life and Work of a Highland Itinerant Missionary," *Scottish Studies* 30 (1991): 59–91.
[33] Stephen J. Hornsby, "Patterns of Scottish Emigration to Canada, 1750–1870," *Journal of Historical Geography* 18 (1992): 398.
[34] Meek, "Independent and Baptist Churches," 277–278.

in 1831,[35] but his reasons appear to have been primarily religious in motivation.

Breadalbane Baptist Church, 1831–1850

Among the Gaelic-speaking Highlanders who landed in Canada after the close of the Napoleonic Wars were a group from the Baptist causes in Killin and Lawers on Loch Tay, Perthshire.[36] The roots of these two churches went back to a large-scale awakening in the Loch Tay district in 1801 and 1802 in which the preaching of a Haldane-trained evangelist by the name of John Farquharson (fl. 1800–1810) was instrumental.[37] Sailing from Greenock on the *Dorothy* on July 12, 1815, only a few weeks after the Battle of Waterloo, these Baptists landed at Montreal after a lengthy voyage. That year they wintered in the southern portion of Glengarry County. The following spring they made their way north to Breadalbane, not far from present-day Dalkeith. A Baptist church was formally organized a year later, on August 2, 1817, with thirteen members and two elders, Allan McDiarmid and Peter McDougall.[38]

By 1829 church membership had grown to about sixty, yet they lacked a pastor who could devote himself fully to ministering to the

---

[35] John Dempsey ("Late Rev. W. Fraser," 8; "William Fraser," 245) and Donald Meek give 1831 as the date of Fraser's emigration to Canada ("Evangelicalism and Emigration," 31). Stuart Ivison and Fred Rosser place his emigration in 1830. See their *The Baptists in Upper and Lower Canada before 1820* (Toronto, ON: University of Toronto Press, 1956), 95. The *Report of the Baptist Home Missionary Society for Scotland, chiefly for the Highlands and Islands*, (1831): 6 seems to indicate that Fraser sailed for British North America in the summer of 1830.

[36] For a study of the faith of this Scottish Baptist community and other Scottish Baptist churches throughout the Ottawa Valley, see Christopher M. Powell, "Scottish Highland Baptist Emigration to the Montreal-Ottawa Region: A Study of the Faith, Practice and Theology of an Immigrant Community, 1816–1900" (Dept of History 2000 Paper, The University of Toronto, 1997).

[37] Meek, "Independent and Baptist Churches," 278–279. For Farquharson, see D. E. Meek, "Farquharson, John" in De S. Cameron, Wright, Lachman, and Meek, ed., *Dictionary of Scottish Church History & Theology*, 316.

[38] Daniel McPhail, *Circular Letter of the Ottawa Baptist Association* (Montreal, QC: J. Starke & Co., 1865), 13. For the history of this congregation, see *Breadalbane Baptist Church History 1816–1991* ([Dalkeith, ON: Breadalbane Baptist Church], 1991).

JESUS, WONDROUS SAVIOUR

needs of the church and reaching out into the surrounding communities with the gospel. The Breadalbane Baptists discovered that John Edwards (1779–1842), a Scotsman from Morayshire who had been converted through the ministry of James Haldane and who had had the oversight of a Baptist work at Clarence on the Ottawa River since the early 1820s,[39] was preparing to sail back to Scotland with the aim of encouraging pastors there to emigrate to eastern Ontario because of the region's great spiritual needs. They asked him to seek out a suitable pastor for their congregation. Edwards sailed for Britain in the autumn of 1829. We know of two that responded positively to his invitation to emigrate: John Gilmour (1792–1869), who came to Montreal in 1830 and organized the first Baptist work there,[40] and Fraser, who settled as the pastor of the Breadalbane church.

William Fraser arrived at Breadalbane in the summer of 1831 and preached his first sermon from the phrase "Escape for thy life" in Genesis 19:17, where Lot and his family are told to flee the city of Sodom and not to look back.[41] Though well received by the congregation, the early years of his ministry at Breadalbane were not easy ones. Since the congregation was not in a position to pay their pastor an adequate salary, Fraser had to teach school for a year or so. He purchased a farm, on which the present church building stands, but since it took some time to clear the land the farm was of little value for a number of years. Thus, Fraser was forced to seek assistance from the New York Baptist Missionary Society.

These financial difficulties were not the worst of his problems, however. What Fraser felt most keenly was the fact that his ministerial

---

[39] For Edwards, see "Biography: Mr. John Edwards," *The Register* 2, no.2 (January 12, 1843): 5–6. *The Register* was published in Montreal.
[40] On Gilmour, see Kenneth Jackson, "Baptist Biographies: John Gilmour," *The Canadian Baptist* (April 1, 1967): 8, 14; Paul R. Dekar, "The Gilmours: Four Generations of Baptist Service" in his and Murray J. S. Ford, ed., *Celebrating the Canadian Baptist Heritage: Three Hundred Years of God's Providence* (Hamilton, ON: McMaster University Divinity College, [1985]), 42–46; *idem*, "Gilmour, John" in Donald M. Lewis, ed., *The Blackwell Dictionary of Evangelical Biography 1730–1860* (Oxford; Cambridge, MA: Blackwell Publishers Ltd., 1995), I, 444.
[41] *Breadalbane Baptist Church History*, 6.

labours seemed to be bearing little fruit. Converts were few and the spiritual life of the church seemed to be ebbing away. In Fraser's own words, "the congregation appeared in a most careless, hardened, and desperate stage."[42] He supposed, he wrote many years later, that "probably all the election of grace were found" in the Breadalbane area and that he "might as well go and seek them on other mountains."[43] In this frame of mind he actually left Breadalbane for a period of time, travelling close to a thousand miles over to Lake Huron and back.[44] By the time that he returned he was convinced he was where God wanted him to be, but this conviction appears to have done little to alleviate his state of despondency.

John Gilmour visited him in the summer of 1834 and sought to encourage his fellow Scotsman. He soon became cognizant, however, that Fraser seemed to have imbibed the notion that praying and preaching for spiritual renewal were utterly useless since this was a sovereign work of God. There must be fire in the pulpit, Gilmour admonished his friend, before there will be a blaze among the congregation. Fraser evidently took this admonition to heart. In his words:

> I betook myself to humiliation, prayer, and fasting; and by solemn inquiry, was astonished to find how full the whole Bible made success depend on God's grace. But not as the Antinomian would have it, and go *to rest*; but would have the true labourer go to work, depending on the Master and His promise for success, as any farmer ever did in his own field, and much more. How evident that God is the life and working power of all the great men of antiquity? Abraham, Isaac, and Jacob; Moses and Joshua; David, Daniel, and all the prophets; and surely the Apostles, under a far more favourable ministration of the Spirit? Now, all this saving power and converting power of God's Spirit is placed in Christ Jesus, as a granary for the supply of the life and labour

---

[42] Letter, October 24, 1834, cited *The Baptist Magazine* 27 (1835): 147. Although this letter is said to be from a "Mr. John Fraser," everything in the letter indicates that William Fraser is its author.
[43] William Fraser, "Sketches of Canadian Baptist Churches. II," *Scottish Baptist Magazine* 4 (1878): 28.
[44] Fraser, "Sketches of Canadian Baptist Churches," 28.

of the church, and will be given to every sincere seeker; and surely His own faithful ministers will not seek it in vain, while they are eminently "co-workers with God" in the work of saving souls, a work which never was meant to be begun or carried on by mere human power.[45]

This text reflects strongly the standpoint of evangelical Calvinism, which had been diffused throughout the nineteenth-century transatlantic Baptist community by the writings of the English Baptist theologian Andrew Fuller (1754–1815).[46] From the vantage-point of this theological system, there are two major errors to be avoided with regard to the Christian life. The first is that of Antinomianism, in which divine grace and Christian freedom are so emphasized that the need for the Christian to follow earnestly after sanctification and to be engaged heartily in evangelism are neglected. The other is moralism, in which the Christian life is viewed primarily as a matter of human will-power and obedience. Rather, Fraser asserts, God's Spirit works in and with Christians, not without them, and thus truly makes them his "co-workers."

---

[45] Fraser, "Sketches of Canadian Baptist Churches," 28.
[46] On Fuller's life, the classic study is that of John Ryland, *The Work of Faith, the Labour of Love, and the Patience of Hope Illustrated; in the Life and Death of the Reverend Andrew Fuller* (London: Button & Son, 1816). A second edition of this biography appeared in 1818. The two best recent biographies are those of Paul Brewster, *Andrew Fuller: Model Pastor–Theologian* (Nashville, TN: B&H Academic, 2010) and Peter J. Morden, *The Life and Thought of Andrew Fuller (1754–1815)* (Milton Keynes, England: Paternoster, 2015).

For brief studies, see Phil Roberts, "Andrew Fuller" in Timothy George and David S. Dockery, ed., *Theologians of the Baptist Tradition*, Rev. ed. (Nashville, TN: Broadman & Holman, 2001), 34–51 and the dictionary article by Michael A.G. Haykin, "Fuller, Andrew" in Timothy Larsen, D.W. Bebbington, and Mark Noll, ed., *Biographical Dictionary of Evangelicals* (Leicester, England: Inter–Varsity Press; Downers Grove, IL: InterVarsity Press, 2003), 241–244. Also see the excellent study by E.F. Clipsham, "Andrew Fuller and Fullerism: A Study in Evangelical Calvinism," *The Baptist Quarterly* 20 (1963–1964): 99–114, 146–154, 214–225, 268–276.

For a good analysis of evangelical Calvinism, see L. G. Champion, "Evangelical Calvinism and the Structures of Baptist Church Life," *The Baptist Quarterly*, 28 (1979-1980), 196-208.

WILLIAM FRASER AND THE BREADALBANE BAPTISTS

Equipped with "these keenly felt convictions" Fraser threw himself back into the work at Breadalbane. His sermons to the unconverted, undergirded by the prayers of the congregation, now impacted the hearts of the hearers with renewing and saving power. That fall and winter there was a large-scale awakening throughout the region around Breadalbane. Similar to the revivals that had swept transatlantic British society in the previous century, the central vehicle in this awakening in the Ottawa Valley was the pulpit. Those who were as "hardened as the flinty rock," to quote what Fraser wrote at the time,

> were made to weep over their sins as little children; almost every house [in the community] has one or more in distress, or rejoicing in the cross of Christ, and the people seem to be smitten with a kind of holy awe, and a respect for divine things. The Lord God of Jacob have all the glory![47]

Between August and December, 1834, Fraser baptized fifty-eight new converts.[48] By the fall of 1835 over one hundred had been converted and brought into the membership of the Breadalbane church.[49] It should be noted that the Breadalbane revival was part of a larger work of the Spirit in the Ottawa Valley. All told some 365 individuals were added to the six Baptist churches of this part of Ontario between August, 1834 and December 1835.[50]

In addition to his ministry in Breadalbane Fraser took an active role in the Ottawa Baptist Association, which had come into existence in 1836 and which consisted of the six churches in the Ottawa Valley and the one in Montreal. Fraser also took extensive preaching tours throughout the Ottawa Valley, often preaching in Gaelic since many of the settlers in this region were from the Highlands. In the Breadalbane church itself Sunday services were held in both Gaelic and English, the services following each other with only a few minutes'

---

[47] Letter, October 24, 1834, cited *Baptist Magazine*, 148.
[48] John Edwards, Letter, January 5, 1835, cited *The Baptist Magazine* 27 (1835): 233.
[49] John Edwards, Letter to J. Neave, January 3, 1836, cited *The Baptist Magazine* 28 (1836): 403; Fraser, "Sketches of Canadian Baptist Churches," 28.
[50] John Edwards, Letter to J. Neave, cited *Baptist Magazine*, 403.

interval. We are told that it was not infrequent for many who heard Fraser preach during this period to be reduced to tears as Fraser warned them of what it meant to be outside of Christ.[51] Many years later a Baptist author by the name of E.R. Fitch would recall Fraser as "a powerful evangelist," whose preaching centred "upon the exceeding sinfulness of sin, the judgments of God and the terrors of the law."[52] For an evangelical Calvinist like Fraser, however, such themes were not an end in themselves. Rather, to quote some remarks made about that quintessential evangelical Calvinist, Jonathan Edwards (1703–1758), preaching on these topics was "part of a larger campaign to turn sinners from their disastrous path and to the rightful object of their affections, Jesus Christ."[53]

---

[51] "Report of the Canada Baptist Missionary Society," *The Canada Baptist Magazine, and Missionary Register* 2, no. 10 (March 1839): 223; "Canada Baptist Missionary Society," *The Canada Baptist Magazine, and Missionary Register* 3, no.8 (February 1840): 188.

[52] E.R. Fitch, *The Baptists of Canada: A History of their Progress and Achievements* (Toronto, ON: The Standard Publishing Co., Ltd., 1911), 105, 171.

[53] John E. Smith, Harry S. Stout, and Kenneth P. Minkema, "Editor's Introduction" in their ed., *A Jonathan Edwards Reader* (New Haven, CT; London: Yale University Press, 1995), xviii.

William Fraser

3

Baptist Polemics

♦ ♦ ♦

DURING WILLIAM FRASER'S sojourn at Breadalbane, he began to be known in Baptist circles as "the ablest controversialist among his brethren."[54] A. H. Newman, a leading nineteenth-century Baptist historian, who made this comment about Fraser, mentioned particularly two polemical pieces by him: one against some of the charismatic followers of Edward Irving (1792–1834) and one against "a rabid opponent of ministerial education."[55] Fraser was also involved in a small controversy with William McKillican (1776–1849), a Scottish Congregationalist minister, over the issue of believer's baptism.

Before he emigrated to Canada, McKillican had pastored the Congregationalist church at Tuar and Acharn, Perthshire, the very locale from which the founders of Breadalbane Baptist church had come.[56] Settling at Breadlabane in 1816, McKillican was soon preaching throughout Glengarry County in both Gaelic and English. In 1838, he clashed with Fraser over the issue of believer's baptism and accused the Baptist of being in "a feverish heat about an ordinance, which, however important in its place, is so distinct from

---

[54] A.H. Newman, "Sketch of the Baptists of Ontario and Quebec to 1851" in D.M. Mihell, ed., *The Baptist Year Book (Historical Number) for Ontario, Quebec, Manitoba and the North-West Territories and British Columbia* (London, ON: The Baptist Convention of Ontario and Quebec, 1900), 77.
[55] Newman, "Sketch of the Baptists of Ontario and Quebec to 1851" 77. The piece against the doctrines of the Scottish preacher Edward Irving may be found in the "Letter from Mr. Fraser to a Preacher of Irvingism," *The Canada Baptist Magazine, and Missionary Register* 1, no. 5 (October, 1837): 97–101. I have been unable to locate the other piece mentioned by Newman.
[56] D.E. Meek, "The Independent and Baptist Churches of Highland Perthshire and Strathspey," *Transactions of the Gaelic Society of Inverness* 56 (1988–1990): 279-280, 323. For an account of McKillican's ministry in Glengarry County, see Donald Neil MacMillan, *The Kirk in Glengarry* (N.p., 1985), 204–208.

real religion, that a *Sorcerer* may submit to it, as well as a *Paul*."[57] Fraser's reply to McKillican was not slow in coming. He denied being consumed with a "feverish heat" with regard to baptism, but did emphasize that McKillican's remark that

> baptism is so distinct from real religion that a sorcerer may submit to it as well as a Paul, is unsound in theology and evil in tendency. It must ... be a part of *real* or of *false* religion; for my part I take it to be a part of the religion of Jesus Christ, as laid down in the New Testament, for our faith and obedience; and Christ crucified is the sum and substance of the ordinance.[58]

In the final remark about the nature of baptism one sees clearly Fraser's voluntarist understanding of Christianity. Only those who can put their trust in the death of Christ for their sins should be baptized.

Despite the fruitfulness of his ministry in the Ottawa Valley, by the end of the 1840s Fraser had come to the conviction that his ministry in Glengarry County was drawing to a close. The membership of the Breadalbane church had declined from 184 in 1838 to 118 in 1849,[59] despite at least one other season of revival in 1840. The decline appears to be mainly due to the fact that many of the members were re-locating in other parts of Ontario, in particular Bruce County, which began to be opened up for settlement in the late 1840s.

Tiverton Baptist Church, 1855–1875

Ever the pioneer church planter, Fraser made the decision to leave Breadalbane in 1850 and head west to Illinois.[60] But he got no further than Bruce County. Initially, he lived on a farm adjoining Kincardine, where he held services in his own home in Gaelic and English. By the

---

[57] William McKillican, "[Letter] To the Editor," *The Canada Baptist Magazine, and Missionary Register* 2 (1838–1839): 10. This letter is in reply to a piece by Fraser: "Mr. Fraser's Visit to Osgood," *The Canada Baptist Magazine, and Missionary Register* 1 (1837–1838): 258–260.

[58] William Fraser, "[Letter] To Mr. M'Killican," *The Canada Baptist Magazine, and Missionary Register* 2 (1838–1839): 62.

[59] "Ottawa Baptist Association," *The Canada Baptist Magazine, and Missionary Register* 1, no. 10 (March, 1838): 232; *The Register* 8, no. 9 (March 1, 1849): [3].

[60] John Dempsey, "William Fraser," *The McMaster University Monthly* 8 (1898–1899): 246.

spring of the following year, though, Fraser was restless. He wrote to John Winterbotham, the pastor of the Baptist church in Woodstock, stating that he was thinking of leaving Kincardine for a place "more eligible for gospel usefulness." Winterbotham suggested he try Owen Sound, where he had just conducted a successful preaching mission.[61]

As it turned out, Fraser moved to what would become Lorne, a hamlet only a few miles to the north of Kincardine along the Lake Huron shoreline. Once settled he erected a sawmill, followed by a grist mill three years later in 1854. Apparently neither of these ventures turned out to be a success.[62] But if he failed in business, the same cannot be said of his preaching and pastoral ministry.

He continued to hold services in Kincardine till 1863, but from the time that he moved to Lorne, he also began to hold services in the home of a fellow Highlander, John Paterson (1805–1883), in the village of Tiverton. Paterson was originally from Tobermory on the Inner Hebridean island of Mull. He had come to Canada in 1831 and settled on a farm in Mariposa township, north of Toronto. In 1851, though, he had re-located to a farm in what would become the village of Tiverton. On Sundays Fraser would walk the five or six miles from his home to that of Paterson, knocking on the doors of all the homes in between, regardless of whether or not they were Baptists. Fraser, said to have "a herculean physical frame,"[63] was probably not an easy man to refuse. Thus, he gathered his congregation as he went!

Tiverton Baptist Church, first known as the Regular Baptist Church of Kincardine and Bruce, was formally constituted with twenty-four members on June 4, 1855. They held their first communion services a few weeks later, on July 1, in the Paterson barn. Over twenty years of ministry, the Tiverton work flourished. Just as Fraser had widely itinerated in the Ottawa Valley, so it was in Bruce County. Often he had to blaze a trail through the woods as he went to preach in towns

---

[61] John Winterbotham, "Mission at Owen Sound," *Christian Observer* 1, no. 5 (May 1851): 74–75. The clause in quotation marks is that of Winterbotham, but he is quoting Fraser.
[62] Dempsey, "William Fraser," 246–247.
[63] Dempsey, "William Fraser," 248.

and villages like Port Elgin, Glammis and North Bruce.[64] When Fraser resigned the pastorate due to age and infirmity in October, 1875, the church membership stood at 354, a figure which would not have included members dismissed to form other Baptist churches in the area or those who might either have died or moved away from the district altogether. While there were a few periods of revival during his ministry at Tiverton, though none it would appear on the scale of that which took place in Breadalbane, much of this growth resulted from Fraser's labours, year in, year out.[65]

After retiring from the ministry at Tiverton, Fraser went to live with his daughter, Mary Ann Coutts (1839–1881), whose husband, James Coutts, was the pastor of the Baptist church in Collingwood. Coutts would later move to Georgetown, where Fraser died on August 30, 1883.

Controversy with Alexander Mackay

Three years before he left the Tiverton pastorate Fraser found himself embroiled in what may well have been the fiercest controversy of his life. Five years after the formal organization of the Baptist church in Tiverton, the Presbyterians in the town had called their first full-time minister, Alexander Mackay (1833–1904), a recent graduate of Knox College, Toronto.[66] Mackay demitted this charge in 1869 to take up a ministry in Illinois. His successor was John Anderson (1823–1908), a native of Strathspey like Fraser.

---

[64] *Tiverton Baptist Church, 1855–1905* ([Tiverton: Tiverton Baptist Church], 1905), 5.
[65] For a mention of one such revival, see *Tiverton Baptist Church*, 5. Throughout this period Ontario Baptists generally continued to be very interested in revival, unlike other denominations such as the Methodists. See M. Richard Mitchell, "A Study of Change Among Ontario's Wesleyans and Baptists, 1840–1900" (MA Thesis, Laurentian University, 1987), 65–76.
[66] On Mackay, see *Knox Church, Tiverton–Ontario: One Hundred Years of Presbyterianism 1859–1959* ([Tiverton: Knox Church, Tiverton], 1959), 8; Kenneth Barker, "Presbyterianism in Grey and Bruce Counties: The Presbyterian Church of Canada (Free) Experience," *Presbyterian History* 38, no.2 (October 1991): 4–5; *idem, Response to Challenge: Presbyterianism In Grey and Bruce* (Owen Sound: n.p., 1995), 10, 25.

During the course of 1872, Mackay was asked to return to Tiverton to deliver two long lectures on the subject of baptism. Peter Cameron, one of the Tiverton Baptist deacons, attended the lectures, which were quite polemical in tone.[67] Apparently Mackay not only attacked the Baptists as a denomination, but even hurled abuse at Fraser by name.[68] Mackay lumped the Baptists together with various groups which many in the nineteenth century, including Baptists, regarded as heterodox, namely, the followers of the German Anabaptist Thomas Müntzer (*c.* 1490–1512), the Mormons, and the Campbellites.[69]

Mackay further suggested that Baptist views about the ordinance of believer's baptism were tantamount to worship of the water and their actual practice of immersing believers quite "indecent"![70] Apart from these inflammatory remarks Mackay spent most of his lectures seeking to demonstrate that baptism in the New Testament era was by "pouring or sprinkling," while baptism by immersion actually could not be found prior to the third century.[71] There appears to have been little substantial argument regarding the subjects of baptism, though Mackay did declare his willingness to "die for infant baptism."[72]

Fraser's reply was two-fold. First, on November 24 he preached a closely-argued sermon on Galatians 3:16 ("Now to Abraham and his seed were the promises made. He saith not, And to seeds, as of many; but as of one, And to thy seed, which is Christ", KJV), in which he rejected the common paedobaptist argument that infant baptism is the New Testament counterpart to circumcision, and that the natural offspring of believers who were so baptized could be assured of salvation. Such a doctrine, he strongly maintained, "has chloroformed

---

[67] Peter Cameron, *The Subject of Baptism: A Reply to the Rev. A. McKay's Lectures at Tiverton, Bruce* (Toronto, ON: Dudley & Burns, 1872), 15. This pamphlet by Cameron was printed together with one by Fraser: *A Historical Sketch of The Baptist Body all the way down from the Apostolic Age* (Toronto, ON: Dudley & Burns, 1872).
[68] Cameron, *Subject of Baptism*, 15.
[69] Cameron, *Subject of Baptism*, 15.
[70] Cameron, *Subject of Baptism*, 17, 18.
[71] Cameron, *Subject of Baptism*, 18–20.
[72] Cameron, *Subject of Baptism*, 21.

millions to live without God, and die in their sins."[73] His argument as a whole was shaped by the voluntarism of the Baptist tradition, though a few of his remarks were particularly noteworthy.

Though there has been ultimately only one way of salvation, Fraser believed that God has carried it out in "three successive, and very different administrations of grace." The first took place during the days of the Patriarchs, when a saving relationship with God was not possible apart from belonging to the extended family of Abraham, Isaac, and Jacob, etc. The second had a national dimension. Instituted at Mount Sinai under Moses, salvation was now linked to one's ethnic status. The final "dispensation" is that of the New Testament, in which people enter into the experience of salvation "as individuals through faith." Only an individual who has personally and sincerely believed in the gospel can have any assurance of salvation. In the words of Fraser: "the door of the church is not wide enough on earth or in heaven for couples, families, or nations, but as individuals."[74] To believe differently from this, in particular to be convinced of the salvific effects of infant baptism, was, from Fraser's standpoint, "pure popery." And to Fraser it seemed as if the Baptists had been specially raised up to demolish what he termed the "Romish pyramid" of infant baptism.[75]

The second item that Fraser prepared in response to Mackay was *A Historical Sketch of the Baptist Body all the way down from the Apostolic Age* (1872). Its basic argument is that the Baptist cause has enjoyed an uninterrupted chronological succession since the Apostolic era. John the Baptist was "the first Baptist" and, according to Fraser, "a people rejecting infant baptism, and holding the immersion of believers in water for baptism" can be traced in the historical record ever since that time.[76] To substantiate this claim Fraser cited a wide variety of groups and individuals. For example, there were the Donatists, who professed

---

[73] William Fraser, *The Covenant of Circumcision as the Ground of Infant Baptism* ([Tiverton: n.p., 1872]), 1–2.
[74] Fraser, *The Covenant of Circumcision* 5–6.
[75] Fraser, *The Covenant of Circumcision* 8.
[76] Fraser, *Historical Sketch*, 1.

"fine Baptist doctrine";[77] Peter de Bruys (d. c.1140), Peter Valdes (d. c.1205–1218), Henry of Lausanne (d. after 1145), Arnold of Brescia (d. 1155), and Berengar of Tours (c.1010–1088), all of them Baptists whose "followers had the same faith";[78] there was even William Tyndale (c.1494–1536), who should be recognized as an important Baptist leader.[79]

This misreading of the historical evidence was, of course, not unique to Fraser. Known as Baptist successionism, it was particularly popular among nineteenth-century North American Baptists. Fraser, it would appear, learned it from G. H. Orchard (1796–1861), an English Baptist minister, whose *A Concise History of Foreign Baptists* (1838) and *A History of the Baptists in England* (1859), proved to be the most influential successionist source in the nineteenth century.[80]

What is unique, though, about Fraser's *Historical Sketch* is the lengthy section that is devoted to showing that the Celtic Church in Britain was actually a Baptist body.[81] This interest in the Celtic Church was obviously linked to the fact that Fraser was a Gaelic speaker. The Celtic Church, he asserts, had "no connections with the state, therefore it was more simple, pure and scriptural in faith and practice." No pastor claimed lordship over another, "for they were all brethren." They rejected infant baptism, a claim that Fraser based on his own observation of a baptistery on the island of Iona. And their long isolation from ecclesial developments on the European continent "naturally served to strengthen and confirm in them the spirit of ecclesiastical freedom."[82]

---

[77] Fraser, *Historical Sketch*, 3–4.
[78] Fraser, *Historical Sketch*, 10.
[79] Fraser, *Historical Sketch*, 11–12.
[80] See Fraser, *Historical Sketch*, 3, where Fraser explicitly cites Orchard.
[81] Fraser, *Historical Sketch*, 6–9. These four pages amount to nearly a quarter of the pamphlet. For two excellent rebuttals of successionism, see W. Morgan Patterson, *Baptist Successionism. A Critical View* (Valley Forge, PA: The Judson Press, 1969), 19–20 and James Edward McGoldrick, *Baptist Successionism: A Crucial Question in Baptist History* (Metuchen, NJ; London: The American Theological Library Association; The Scarecrow Press, Inc., 1994).
[82] Fraser, *Historical Sketch*, 6, 8.

Although this idealized portrait of the Celtic Church distorts the real nature of Celtic Christianity, it does say much about Fraser's own convictions at this late period in his life. His voluntaristic vision of the Baptist life, learned first in the Strathspey, then tested and refined in the crucible of ministry in the Scottish Highlands and in the Ottawa Valley, appears to have diminished not a whit during his days in Tiverton.

Benjamin Davies

4

Canada Baptist College and Benjamin Davies

♦ ♦ ♦

IT HAS BEEN ONE of the greatest privileges of my life to serve the evangelical Baptist churches of Ontario through the medium of theological education. Like other areas of vocational ministry, it has not been without its challenges, one of which has been the lackadaisical attitude towards formal theological education on the part of far too many Baptist congregations in the province. Historically, though, this attitude has deep roots in Ontario Baptist soil. While Methodists and Presbyterians in what would become Ontario recognized the importance of having a theological college early on, it would not be until 1860, nearly eighty years after Baptists had first come into Ontario that they would have a successful school for training pastors, what was known as the Canadian Literary Institute in Woodstock.

Canada Baptist College

Now, there had been an earlier attempt to fund such a school, Canada Baptist College in Montreal, but it had failed in 1849 after only eleven years of operation. This school had its origins in the earliest days of the Ottawa Association, when, in 1836, it recommended that an academy be established in either Upper or Lower Canada to train men for the Baptist ministry.[83] That very year John Gilmour, the Scottish Baptist pastor of First Baptist Church, Montreal, sailed to England to seek to raise support for a possible seminary. His trip was not in vain, for Gilmour returned in March, 1837, with between £1500–£1600

---

[83] A.H. Newman, "Sketch of the Baptists of Ontario and Quebec to 1851," *The Baptist Year Book (Historical Number)* (1900): 80.

(probably close to $880,000 in today's currency) for an educational institution.[84]

A number of sites for the new college were considered. Eventually a site in Montreal was chosen, possibly because it was the centre of British banking and business interests. Thus, on September 24, 1838, Canada Baptist College opened its doors in Montreal with two students.[85] The school curriculum was curious in some ways. For instance, along with the biblical languages, Hebrew and Greek, the students were also taught Latin, Syriac, and German, but not French, even though the school was situated in Montreal!

Its first principal was Benjamin Davies (1814–1875), a Welsh Baptist scholar, who had secured a PhD from the University of Leipzig in 1838 when he was only twenty-four. The first PhD in a Canadian institution of higher learning, he directed the school from 1838 to 1843.[86] During his five years at the school roughly thirty students benefited from his teaching and counsel.[87] In a circular letter that Davies drew up for the Ottawa Association in 1840, the Baptist educator provides a concise overview of his view of theological education.[88] It is an overview that is still instructive.

A perspective on theological education

Deep distrust of theological education has long been endemic among Baptists. In the mid-eighteenth century, for example, the deacons of the Baptist cause in Westbury Leigh, Wiltshire, England, viewed

---

[84] Newman, "Sketch of the Baptists," 81–82.

[85] For the story of the school, see George W. Campbell, "Canada Baptist College, 1838–1849. The Generation and Demise of a Pioneering Dream in Canadian Theological Education" (MTh thesis, Knox College, University of Toronto, 1974). See also "Canada Baptist College (1836–1849)" (http://web.ncf.ca/fm120/History/Bosworth/Canada Baptist College (1836-1849).htm; accessed May 1, 2023).

[86] On Davies, see J.H.Y. Briggs, "Davies, Benjamin" in Donald M. Lewis, ed., *The Blackwell Dictionary of Evangelical Biography 1730–1860* (Oxford; Cambridge, MA: Blackwell Publishers Ltd., 1995), 1:295.

[87] *Montreal Register* 3 (February 22, 1844): 2.

[88] For the entire circular letter, see Appendix 1.

human learning in a pastor with feelings of suspicion, and entertained the strongest aversion to those whom they termed "men-made" ministers. ... The Bristol Academy ... presented the nearest object of mistrust to the members at Westbury Leigh. ... They could never bring themselves to regard this seat of human learning with any degree of complacency; and they scorned, as they said, "to go down to Egypt for help."[89]

A similar attitude was discernible among Ontario Baptists in the mid-nineteenth century. As Davies wrote, "it is to be feared there are some, who look upon it [i.e. theological education] with jealousy, if not with hostility."[90]

Seeking to disarm this hostility, Davies pointed out first of all that the support of formal theological education in no way entailed the belief that "none can be worthy and useful ministers without education." In fact, there were a good number of examples to the contrary in the history of the church. The early Apostles were an eminent example in this regard. Nevertheless, Davies argued, the reason why such uneducated individuals succeed is either because they labour among "people as uncultivated as themselves" or they possess "natural powers of mind." Illustrative of the latter was John Bunyan (1628–1688), who, though an "untutored tinker," had a natural genius which made of him "a mighty preacher and an immortal author." In fact, Davies was quick to point out, there were many uneducated ministers who "are often heard lamenting their deficiencies, and coveting learning as a help to them in their work." Davies saw a good example in this regard in another English Baptist, Andrew Fuller, "of blessed memory, who began to preach when very unlearned, but who was so sensible of his disadvantages that he used great diligence to acquire that knowledge, without which he could never be, what he at

---

[89] John Clark Marshman, *The Life and Times of Carey, Marshman and Ward* (London: Longman, Brown, Green, Longmans, & Roberts, 1859), 1:105–106.
[90] Benjamin Davies, "Ministerial Education," *The Canada Baptist Magazine* 3, no.9 (March, 1840): 193.

length became, one of the most valuable men of his time, and decidedly the most useful minister in our religious community."[91]

On the other hand, not for a moment did Davies believe that "education alone, apart from moral adaptation, can qualify for the ministry."[92] Responding to those who were coming to regard ministerial training in the same terms as training for any other profession, Davies vehemently asserted:

> It is a notorious fact, that in all secular or state churches, young men are raised to undertake 'the care of souls,' without any regard to their religious feelings. We however utterly reprobate such a notion and such a custom. Much as we desire a *learned* ministry, we desire a *pious* ministry more. The first and most essential qualification, which we look for and demand, is godliness, while we seek learning only as a secondary, though not unimportant preparation. It is our solemn conviction that no literary attainments, no powers of rhetoric, can give fitness for the work, if the heart be not engaged in it. This preparation of the heart in man must come from the Lord, before any other preparation, whether of erudition or of eloquence, can qualify him for the ministry.[93]

In training a person for pastoral ministry learning, though important, is not as vital as piety. It is the latter—the engagement of the heart, the longing for holiness, the love of human beings—which is absolutely indispensable in a pastor's life. And this piety is itself God's creation. In other words, unlike other professions, genuine pastoral ministry must arise from a calling from God.

The necessity of a college

In seeking to raise support for Canada Baptist College, a place of formal study, Davies had no intention of casting aspersions on other, more informal methods of education. "If the learning itself be sound and to the purpose," he rightly noted, "we care not much whether it has been gained at home, or in the collegiate seats of liberal education,

---

[91] Davies, "Ministerial Education," 194–195.
[92] Davies, "Ministerial Education," 195.
[93] Davies, "Ministerial Education," 195–196.

or in the halls of divinity." Davies could point to a number of self-taught men in the transatlantic Baptist community which amply demonstrated his point:

> Who does not know the history of our illustrious [William] Carey, how he became a prodigy of teaming, without having ever frequented the groves of Academus? How happy a circumstance would it be for the cause of truth, if unlettered ministers generally were to follow the bright example of Carey, Fuller, [Abraham] Booth and others, by struggling through their difficulties and placing themselves on a level with the well instructed and enlightened![94]

But Davies was a realist and knew that the achievements of a William Carey or an Andrew Fuller were probably too much to expect of most men. A theological college was thus a necessity.

Among the goals of such an institution Davies noted two in particular. First, a formal theological education will "greatly assist" budding pastors "in studying and understanding the Scriptures." Without a doubt, what the Bible has to say about "the way of salvation and the principal duties incumbent on man" is easy to understand. Yet, even the apostle Peter had to admit that in Paul's writings there are "some things hard to be understood, which they that are unlearned and unstable wrest, as they do also the other scriptures, unto their own destruction" [2 Peter 3:16 (KJV)].

A close reading of the Scriptures reveals other areas of difficulty. As Davies noted, though, this should not be considered surprising.

> A collection of writings, that are of such high antiquity, several of them being the most ancient in existence, that were composed by Orientals for the use, in the first place, of people, whose mode of living, thinking, and speaking differed widely from our own, that treat on the most sublime and abstruse subjects, and that too in languages which have long since ceased to be spoken, and therefore not easily mastered, and that have been handed down for many generations by the labor of the pen, which is a process far less favorable to correctness than printing—surely a collection of such a character, must be expected to contain parts,

---

[94] Davies, "Ministerial Education," 196.

exceedingly obscure to us, however clear they may have been to the first readers.[95]

Understanding the cultural, intellectual, and linguistic differences between the world in which the Bible was written and nineteenth-century British North America, as well as having some cognizance of the various difficulties posed by the transmission of the biblical text, required theological education if the text was to be faithfully proclaimed to Canadians. Nor can a preacher simply trust commentaries to relieve him of his difficulties. If he does, he is at the mercy of those who write them. "Every professed and public expounder of the lively oracles," Davies averred, should "desire and…be able to form an enlightened and matured opinion" of the texts on which he is speaking. Davies pointed out that this would obviously entail some understanding of the original languages, a further reason for formal training.[96]

A second major reason why education was needed was to enable ministers to be more effective in their explanation of God's Word to others. A good theological training helps those who are to be ministers to present their beliefs intelligibly, cogently, and in a winsome fashion. It enables them to order their sermons so that they do "not present a confused mass of ideas, jumbled together without connection and without design." Davies was well aware that the age in which he lived was one in which various "learned criticisms" were being advanced against the truths of the Scriptures. How could the Bible be defended, though, without some education?[97]

Davies closed with a fervent appeal.

> Having thus, beloved brethren, laid before you the subject of ministerial education, we cannot close without affectionately urging you to support the theological institution, [Canada Baptist College,] now established among us. Will you permit it to decline and fall, by withholding from it your prayers and contributions? Will those who have the means to provide education for pious

---

[95] Davies, "Ministerial Education," 197.
[96] Davies, "Ministerial Education," 197–198.
[97] Davies, "Ministerial Education," 198–199.

and gifted young men, who thirst for improvement, deny them any assistance? Unfaithfulness in this matter must be positive treachery to the cause.[98]

By and large, though, Davies' appeal fell on deaf ears.

The closing of Canada Baptist College

Davies was replaced by John Mockett Cramp (1796–1881),[99] also a British Baptist, who served as principal till the College folded in 1849. Since Davies was a vocal open communionist, it has been common to attribute the demise of the school to the conflict between open and closed communionists. This is certainly one reason for the school's failure. For instance, one of the earliest associations of Baptist churches in Ontario, the Clinton Conference, which was formally a part of the powerful Shaftesbury Association of Vermont, New York, and New Hampshire until 1819, had a strong commitment to a closed communion polity. The statement of faith of one of the churches in this association, Charlotteville (Vittoria), which was founded in 1803, specified that "none have a right" to participate in the Lord's Supper but those "have been duly baptized" as believers and "received into the church."[100] But this theological conflict was not the only cause for the school's demise.

In 1849 Montreal was in the grip of a severe depression and that year there was a major cholera outbreak in the city, both of which discouraged potential students from coming to the College. The school had also been receiving support from British Baptist sources, but by 1849 this had completely dried up. Finally, there was the

---

[98] Davies, "Ministerial Education," 200.
[99] On Cramp, see Robert S. Wilson, "Cramp, John Mockett" in Lewis, ed., *Blackwell Dictionary of Evangelical Biography*, 1:266.
[100] Cited William Norman Albert Gillespie, "Ontario's 19th Century Baptist Tradition: Its Roots and its Development" (PhD thesis, University of Waterloo, 1990), 131–132. The Vittoria church had the oldest continuous existence of all of the Baptist churches in Ontario until June 2013, when the twenty members of the Church voted to disband. See Monte Sonnenberg, "Vittoria Baptists vote to disband", *Simcoe Reformer* (Tuesday, July 30, 2013) (http://www.simcoereformer.ca/2013/07/30/vittoria-baptists-vote-to-disband; accessed June 8, 2023).

geographical isolation of the College from the bulk of the churches it was supposed to serve. Most of this constituency was between three to six hundred miles away to the west. It was impractical to expect ministerial students to journey that far in a day when transportation was exhausting and costly. For example, when John Girdwood, the pastor of the First Baptist Church in Montreal, traveled from Perth to Montreal in 1842, he had to "catch a stage at four a.m., travel over bone-shaking roads for many hours, then transfer to a river-boat to reach Montreal, the total journey occupying thirty-six hours."[101] The usual travelling time for a stage-coach from Toronto to Montreal was between ninety and one hundred hours!

Finally, nineteenth-century Baptist individualism played a role in the closure of Canada Baptist College. Especially under the impress of the writings of influential theologians like the American Baptist Francis Wayland (1796–1865), Baptists in Ontario, like their cousins in the United States, began to lose touch with the early connectionalism which held Baptists together in associations in both the British Isles and colonial America, a connectionalism that made possible co-operation in theological education. Instead, the contention began to be made that local churches are independent democracies and that "it was both wrong and dangerous to speak of the "interdependence" of churches."[102] As one Baptist later said in 1853 about the negative impact that this rugged individualism had had upon early Baptist life in Ontario:

> Had the Baptist of Canada laid aside their mutual jealousies at an earlier day, and concentrated their strength in aggressive movements upon the domains of sin and error, not only would our denominational statistics have reached a higher figure, but

---

[101] Theo T. Gibson, *Robert Alexander Fyfe: His Contemporaries and His Influence* (Burlington, ON: Welch Publishing Co., 1998), 72.
[102] Norman H. Maring, "The Individualism of Francis Wayland" in Winthrop Still Hudson, ed., *Baptist Concepts of the Church: A Survey of the Historical and Theological Issues which Have Produced Changes in Church Order* (Philadelphia, PA: Judson Press, 1959), 136.

what is of infinitely more importance, Christ would have been more honoured by us...[103]

With the closure of Canada Baptist College, it would be a dozen years before the Ontario Baptist churches had another school of their own. The founding principal of that second school, the Canadian Literary Institute, would face similar challenges to Davies, but thankfully times were changing and the necessity of the school was increasingly recognized by Baptists in Ontario as the century wore on. Davies' reasons for having such a school, though, would remain as valid in the late nineteenth century as they were in 1840. And this author deems them to be still wisdom as we seek both "a learned" and "a pious ministry."

---

[103] "Regular Baptist Missionary Society," *The Christian Observer* 3, no.11 (November 1853): 168.

Robert Alexander Fyfe

5

Robert Alexander Fyfe and the Canadian Literary Institute

♦ ♦ ♦

CANADIANS, IT HAS BEEN SAID, do not relish heroes. Quite differently from those peoples who have played major roles in shaping our national character—the French, British and Americans—our history has given us a predilection for the ordinary. We have never had such hero-producing events as a revolution or a national revival. Great Britain, France, and the United States have all experienced the former and the larger-than-life figures those revolutions produced. The nearest we have come to such have been the rebellions of 1837, which, as Charles Taylor has noted, "are notable mainly for their ineptitude."[104] Nor has there ever been a national revival. Both the British Isles and America have known the blessing of such, while France experienced the extraordinary impact of the gospel during the period of the Reformation, when the Reformed faith grew from a handful of believers in the early 1520s to two million or so by the late 1560s. To be sure, we have had local revivals like the one in Newfoundland between 1766 and 1773 or that in the Ottawa Valley in the mid-1830s. The closest we have come to anything on a much larger scale was when the Maritimes were radically transformed through the preaching of Henry Alline (1748–1784), "the soul-ravishing evangelist and hymnist whose personal impact was unforgettable."[105]

---

[104] Charles Taylor, *Six Journeys: A Canadian Pattern* (Toronto, ON: House of Anansi Press Ltd., 1977), i. The first couple of paragraphs are indebted to Taylor's observations in his "Introduction" to this book.
[105] D.G. Bell, *Henry Alline and Maritime Religion* (Ottawa, ON: The Canadian Historical Association, 1993), 18.

In fact, when a potentially great figure emerges among us, we are quick to trivialize them and focus on their flaws and blunders. Taylor instances the way we have dealt with our first Prime Minister, John A. MacDonald (1815–1891), or with the more recent political figure, John G. Diefenbaker (1895–1979).[106] In Canadian church history, one need only think of the way that the memory of T.T. Shields (1873–1955) has fared.[107] Yet, as Taylor also observes, it is clear that "we have produced some remarkable people whose qualities often verge on the heroic."[108] In the history of the Baptist community in Ontario during the second half of the nineteenth century this is most definitely the case. There we find such remarkable men as the subject of this chapter, Robert Alexander Fyfe (1816–1878), who had an enormous impact upon the shape and direction of the Baptist denomination in Ontario and Quebec.

Becoming R.A. Fyfe

Robert Alexander Fyfe was born in Laprairie, Quebec in 1816, the son of Scottish immigrants who had emigrated from Dundee seven years earlier.[109] His father James was a Presbyterian—though later to become a Baptist in 1846—and his mother a Baptist. Little has been preserved regarding the home in which Fyfe grew up, though one gets a flavour of his mother's strength of character and piety in an anecdote recorded by Fyfe's first biographer, his lifelong friend J.E. Wells. It seems that Mrs. Fyfe was lamenting to a friend on one occasion about a number of dissensions that were then racking the local Baptist

---

[106] Taylor, *Six Journeys*, ii.
[107] For Shields, see Chapter 11.
[108] Taylor, *Six Journeys*, ii.
[109] On Fyfe's life, see especially J. E. Wells, *Life and Labors of Robert Alex. Fyfe, D.D.* (Toronto, ON, [1885]) and Theo T. Gibson, *Robert Alexander Fyfe: His Contemporaries and His Influence* (Burlington, ON: Welch Publishing Co., 1988). Details of his life mentioned below are drawn from one or these sources. For a concise study, see also F. T. Rosser, "Fyfe, Robert Alexander," *Dictionary of Canadian Biography*, ed. Marc Le Terreur (Toronto: University of Toronto Press, 1972), X, 295–296. Fyfe recalled aspects of his life and ministry in *A Forty Years' Survey from Bond Street Pulpit* (Toronto, ON, 1876).

church of which she was a member. Her friend asked her why she didn't leave such a "quarrelsome church" and join another Baptist work located nearby that was known for its pacific character. "Oh!" Mrs. Fyfe answered, "the members of that church don't know enough to quarrel."[110]

When exactly Fyfe was converted is not known. Later in life Fyfe said little about the details surrounding his conversion. Theo T. Gibson, his last major biographer, reasons that Fyfe "seems to have regarded this transforming experience…as too sacred a subject for much talk, at the same time affirming constantly that such an event was utterly essential and had, in fact, taken place in him."[111] He was subsequently baptized in the St. Lawrence on April 27, 1835, by John Gilmour. Conscious of a call to vocational ministry Fyfe went to study at the Hamilton Literary and Theological Institution in New York, then situated about half-way between Albany and Buffalo. He returned to Ontario soon after his graduation in 1842 and pastored initially in Perth, then later in Toronto at March Street Baptist Church from 1844 to 1848. Originally organized in 1818, March Street was the first Baptist work in Toronto, then called York.[112] After a period of ministry in the United States Fyfe returned to Toronto in 1855 to take up again the pastorate of the congregation that he had pastored in the 1840s. In the time he had been gone, the church had relocated to Bond Street and was accordingly now known as Bond Street Baptist Church.

During this second Toronto pastorate Fyfe emerged as one of the key leaders of the Baptist community in Ontario. In 1859 he assumed the ownership of the *Christian Messenger*, the main Baptist newspaper of Ontario. The following year he renamed it as *The Canadian Baptist* and used its columns to disseminate and persuade others of his vision of the Baptist cause and its future in Ontario. For instance, in the issue for December 15, 1859, Fyfe was critical of the embrace by C.H.

---

[110] Wells, *Life and Labors of Robert Alex. Fyfe*, 19.
[111] Gibson, *Robert Alexander Fyfe*, 14.
[112] For the history of this church, see Michael A.G. Haykin with Roy M. Paul, ed., *Set for the Defense of the Gospel: A Bicentennial History of Jarvis Street Baptist Church, 1818–2018* (Toronto, ON: Jarvis Street Baptist Church, 2018).

Spurgeon (1834-1892) of open communion, that is, allowing those who were considered unbaptized believers to partake of the Lord's Supper. As we saw at the close of the previous chapter, the Ontario Baptist community was divided by disputes over this issue and these disputes, at times quite acerbic, had done much to hinder their growth. Spurgeon was having a growing influence upon the North American Baptist scene and Fyfe, a closed communionist who held that only baptized believers should partake of the Lord's Supper, was possibly fearful that Spurgeon's views might lead to greater fissiparousness among Baptists in Ontario. He thus did not hesitate to argue that the "unscripturalness" of Spurgeon's view virtually endorsed the error of the Paedopbaptist position.[113] It is interesting to note that many years later, in 1874, while on vacation in England, he went to hear Spurgeon preach and revelled in the English Baptist's preaching.[114]

The Canadian Literary Institute

Like a number of other Ontario Baptist pastors Fyfe was also deeply exercised about the lack of a facility for theological and higher education among Baptists in his native province. On November 19, 1856, owing in part to Fyfe's leadership, a Baptist convention had convened in Brantford to make some concrete decisions about this matter. Among the decisions made that day was one that called for the establishment of a school to be located neither "east of St. Catherines" nor "west of London."[115] Within a month it had been decided to locate the school in Woodstock on property provided by a Baptist deacon, Archibald Burtch.[116]

This school became a reality in the summer of 1860 when, as the Canadian Literary Institute, it formally opened with seventy-nine students and five teachers. In a report that was drawn up with regard

---

[113] Gibson, *Robert Alexander Fyfe*, 242–243, 340.
[114] Gibson, *Robert Alexander Fyfe*, 301.
[115] "What was done at the Convention?," *The Christian Messenger* 3, no.9 (November 27, 1856): 2, cols. 2–3 and "Baptist Educational Convention," *The Christian Messenger* 3, no.9 (November 27, 1856): 2, cols. 7–8.
[116] "R.A. Fyfe, W. Wilkinson, and Hoyes Lloyd, "Location of the Baptist Institute," *The Christian Messenger* 3, no.13 (December 25, 1856): 2, col. 7.

to the 1856 convention that had led directly to the building of this school, the Baptist leadership behind the school were hopeful that they had "entered upon a new and more prosperous era in the history of our denomination in Canada."[117] They were right. Ontario Baptists had indeed entered upon a new, and far more fruitful, phase of their history. And much of that fruitfulness was linked to the school at Woodstock. It is not fortuitous, therefore, that the motto of the school—given to it by Fyfe—was *Sit Lux*, "Let there be light."[118]

Not surprisingly, Fyfe was asked to head up the school as its first principal. He resigned from the Bond Street pulpit in mid-March 1860 and by mid-June was in Woodstock. He had come from a demanding and busy pastorate and he had no time for rest before assuming the challenge of his new position. As he wrote to an old friend, Daniel McPhail (1811–1874), who has been remembered as "the Elijah of the Ottawa Valley" because of the power of his preaching and prayers:

> The confidence which my brethren in the ministry have, almost to a man, expressed in me as Principal, has affected me in a manner beyond my power to describe. While it encourages me, it makes me tremble. Who is sufficient to mould and train our rising ministry? I hope you and the ministry generally, as well as the churches generally, will remember me at the Throne of Grace. Will you not have some set time, some monthly season, of prayer for God's blessing on the Institute? …
>
> I love to preach the Gospel. I love to recall the times—now far in the past—when you and I visited many destitute fields together. And if I had my own way, I would ask no better work than to be without pastoral charge, with enough to live upon. Let me go from place to place and seek out 'the few sheep in the wilderness.' One of the considerations which induce me to go to Woodstock, is that I shall still have opportunities to preach.
>
> I should be glad if I could get a few days or weeks rest, before entering upon my new duties, for I feel weary and my toils and

---

[117] "What was done at the Convention?," 2, cols, 2–3.
[118] Gibson, *Robert Alexander Fyfe*, 343.

anxieties for the past year have been very great. But I fear I shall get no rest.[119]

Fyfe's fear was well-founded. The school grew to a peak of 253 students by 1874 and was enormously influential in giving shape and cohesion to the Baptist cause in Ontario. Some of the key leaders of the late nineteenth-century Baptist community in Ontario, like E.W. Dadson (1845–1900), and this community's first overseas missionaries, John McLaurin (1839–1912) and Americus Vespucius Timpany (1840–1885), were students under Fyfe.[120] But leadership of the school took a heavy toll on Fyfe. Every school year between 1861 and his death in 1878 from diabetic complications, Fyfe regularly taught six hours a day, five days a week. On Sundays he never declined an opportunity to preach and conduct Sunday School classes. And in the summers, he would travel the length of the province raising funds for the school. In the entire seventeen years that he was principal he only took two vacations and all but worked himself to death.

Controversy over open and closed communion

To add to the stress of these years he was a vigorous participant in a couple of controversies that were ultimately rooted in the communion issue. Among his main opponents were sadly his old friend Daniel McPhail and the key figures of the Grande Ligne Mission in Quebec, Henrietta Feller (1800–1868) and Louis Roussy (d.1881). By the time of these controversies, the Grande Ligne Mission, which had begun its work in Quebec in the 1830s, had successfully planted twenty preaching points in the province and had seen around 3,000 converts. The Mission, though, was open communion, and Fyfe maintained that only those organizations that were closed communion merited financial support from closed communionists, then called Regular Baptists. This use of the adjective "Regular" indicated that the church observed the ordinances in the "regular order," that is, those partaking of the Lord's Supper had to have been baptized as believers by

---

[119] Cited Wells, *Life and Labors of Robert Alex. Fyfe*, 309.
[120] For an estimation of Fyfe's impact in this regard, see Gibson, *Robert Alexander Fyfe*, 274–278.

immersion. As Theo Gibson has observed, "there were no winners in the Grande Ligne controversy, but incalcuable losses." The Francophone Baptist Mission was cut off from the funding of most Regular Baptist works in Ontario and the result was that many French Canadian towns and villages went unevangelized. Gibson describes Fyfe's role in this controversy as the "acknowledged bell-wether of the Regular Baptists" and suggests that Fyfe may have become so "obsessed with the need to keep Regular Baptists together that he became one-track in promoting their distinctives."[121]

Here Fyfe failed to emulate the example of two of the key founders of the English Baptist Missionary Society, a missionary society that he deeply admired. During their lives, those two founders, Andrew Fuller and John Ryland, Jr. (1753–1825), were at opposite ends of the spectrum on this volatile issue of who should take the Lord's Supper in a Baptist Church. Fuller adhered to a policy of closed membership—that is, only baptized believers could become members of the church that pastored—and closed communion. Ryland, on the other hand, was of the conviction that both the Lord's Supper and membership in the local church should be open to all Christians, regardless of whether or not they had been baptized as believers. He was thus committed to a policy of both open communion and open membership. Yet, Fuller and Ryland did not allow their disagreement on this matter to affect their friendship.[122] They obviously recognized that this subject was not the all-essential issue that many of their Baptist acquaintances—as well as Fyfe and many among the Ontario Baptists decades later—thought it was. Fuller and Ryland thus displayed a model of wisdom and maturity for Baptists in every time and context.

---

[121] Gibson, *Robert Alexander Fyfe*, 298.
[122] For further discussion of the import of the friendship of Fuller and Ryland, see Michael A.G. Haykin, *Iron Sharpens Iron: Friendship and the grace of God* (Bridgend, Wales: Union Publishing, 2022).

William McMaster

6

John Harvard Castle and William McMaster

◆ ◆ ◆

ONE OF THE results of the War of 1812–1814 was that Canadians strongly aligned themselves with the British Empire throughout the nineteenth century and saw themselves as an integral part of that imperial world. So, Ontario Baptists naturally turned more often to Great Britain than to the United States if they were seeking pastors for their pulpits. The coming of the American Baptist John Harvard Castle (1830–1890) to take on the pastorate of Bond Street Baptist Church in Toronto in 1873 was thus a little out of the ordinary.[123] Yet, Castle was only a second-generation American. His family were Scots-Irish who emigrated to Pennsylvania in 1825. Converted under the ministry of J. Lansing Burrows (1814–1893)[124] and baptized as a believer when he was 16, he soon sensed a call to pastoral ministry. To prepare

---

[123] For the life of Castle, see especially Thomas Trotter, "John Harvard Castle," *McMaster University Monthly*, 1 (1891–1892): 145–150; Charles M. Johnston, "Castle, John Harvard," *Dictionary of Canadian Biography*, 11 (University of Toronto; Université Laval, 2003–2018); http://www.biographi.ca/en/bio/castle_john_harvard_11E.html; accessed May 2, 2023).

See also B.D. Thomas, "Pulpit and Platform. 'A Servant of His Age' " (Newspaper clipping in B.D. Thomas, "My Pastorate in Toronto" [Scrapbook of newspaper clippings, McMaster Divinity College Archives, McMaster University, Hamilton, Ontario]). This is a memorial sermon for Castle based on Acts 13:30 and given at Jarvis Street by his successor, B.D. Thomas, on June 22, 1890. At the end of it there is a biographical sketch of Castle. Thomas commenced this scrapbook of newspaper cuttings about his ministry, his sermons, and Jarvis Street Baptist Church when he came to Toronto in the autumn of 1882, but it also contains items from earlier phases of his ministry.

[124] On Burrows, see William Cathcart, "Burrows, John Lansing, D.D.," *The Baptist Encyclopaedia* (Philadelphia, PA: Louis H. Everts, 1883), 169.

himself to that end, Castle first studied at the newly-founded University at Lewisburg (now Bucknell University), which had been established by members of White Deer Valley Baptist Church who deemed it "desirable that a Literary Institution should be established in Central Pennsylvania, embracing a High School for male pupils, another for females, a College and also a Theological Institution."[125] Castle was part of the first graduating class in 1851.

His studies then took him to Rochester Theological Seminary in upstate New York for two years. Following graduation from Rochester, he was ordained at Pottsville, Pennsylvania, in 1853, where he pastored for two and a half years. From there he went on to serve another pastorate in Newburgh, New York, where he met Sarah Moulton Fraser (1819–1916), a devout Connecticut-born Baptist once described as "a woman of strong character,"[126] who would be instrumental in bringing Castle to pastor Bond Street Baptist Church, where R.A. Fyfe had faithfully served two terms as pastor. After the death of Moulton's first husband, James Fraser, the American widow had married William McMaster (1811–1887) in 1871. McMaster was an Irish immigrant from County Tyrone in Ulster, who arrived in Toronto in 1833 and soon became a partner in, and then sole proprietor of, a dry goods firm. Concentrating his energies on wholesaling, he became one of the wealthiest men in Toronto by the 1850s, whereupon he entered into banking. He subsequently helped found the Canadian Bank of Commerce in 1867, and as its first president built it into the leading bank in Ontario.[127]

---

[125] "The University's Founding" (https://www.bucknell.edu/x1176.xml; accessed October 6, 2018).

[126] Charles J. Holman, "Susan Moulton McMaster," *The McMaster University Monthly* 26, no.4 (January, 1917): 143–144. Holman noted that Susan's four sisters as well as her mother and father were eventually won to the Baptist cause by Susan's witness (Holman, "Susan Moulton McMaster," 143).

[127] On McMaster, see especially D.E. Thomson, "William McMaster," *McMaster University Monthly* 1 (1891–1892): 97–103; Charles M. Johnston, *McMaster University: Volume 1/The Toronto Years* (Toronto, ON; Buffalo; NY: University of Toronto Press for McMaster University, 1976), 18–50; Charles M. Johnston,

JOHN HARVARD CASTLE & WILLIAM McMASTER

McMaster had been one of the earliest members of the church, joining during its March Street days. During the height of his business success, it was said that there were those who thought him "dull in not perceiving that his business and social welfare would have been greatly promoted by his union with one of the larger and stronger bodies" of Christians, like the Methodists, Presbyterians, or Anglicans. When McMaster joined the Toronto Baptists, there was little doubt that it was a seemingly small, insignificant body. But as John Castle said of McMaster after the latter's death: "In his early life the denomination to which he belonged was in these Provinces an obscure one. But with a fidelity which never faltered he identified himself most thoroughly with the people who held truth as he understood truth."[128]

Castle comes to Bond Street

When William Stewart resigned from the pastorate of Bond Street in May of 1872,[129] Susan Moulton McMaster encouraged the congregation to consider her former pastor, John Castle, who was then pastoring in Philadelphia.[130] Members of the pulpit committee went to Philadelphia in November of 1872 where they heard Castle preach. They "were favorably impressed both by his sermons and by the high regard and esteem in which he was held by the members of the church and by other ministering brethren" in the area.[131] They thus encouraged the church to extend an invitation to him to assume the church's pastorate. The church unanimously voted to call Castle and it was specified that his salary would not exceed $3,000.[132] Three weeks

---

Wendy Cameron, *et al.*, "McMaster, William," *Dictionary of Canadian Biography*, vol. 11 (University of Toronto/Université Laval, 2003–2018; http://www.biographi.ca/en/bio/mcmaster_william_11E.html; accessed October 6, 2018). See also Holman, "Susan Moulton McMaster," 146.

[128] Cited Thomson, "William McMaster," 98.

[129] "Jarvis Street Baptist Church Minute Book 1866–1881," Minute of May 13, 1872 (Jarvis Street Baptist Church Archives, Toronto, ON).

[130] Holman, "Susan Moulton McMaster," 144.

[131] "Jarvis Street Baptist Church Minute Book 1866–1881," Minute of November 24, 1872.

[132] "Jarvis Street Baptist Church Minute Book 1866–1881," Minute of November 24, 1872.

later Castle replied by telegram that he was prepared to accept the call. He also sent a letter which was read to the church on December 23 in which he expressed his conviction that the "guidance of the Divine Spirit" had been "humbly and earnestly sought" by the Toronto Baptists. He believed that they had had "only the glory of Christ in view" in inviting him to be their pastor. After prayer and consultation with a number of fellow pastors, whom Castle described as loving "the Kingdom of Christ more than any one local church," Castle felt bound to accept the call as God's will for his and his family's life. And so he was prepared now, as he put it, "to leave my native city and seek a home among strangers in a strange land."

Castle stressed that he did not "intend to do great things in coming" to Toronto, "for this is not in me," he said. But he did expect that God would use "an humble, praying, harmonious church, united in its pastor, to secure great blessings for itself, for the city and country in which it is placed, and even for distant nations."[133] It is noteworthy that the way Castle described the church here is in strong contrast to its early years, during which there had been significant division and disharmony and, in the words of Castle's successor, Benjamin Daniel Thomas (1843–1917), the number of members being small and the location of their first building on the northeast corner of Lombard and Church Streets not being the best, it "put all real progress amongst the impossibilities." The church thus had a "very checkered career" during its first decades of existence.[134] Castle's coming to Toronto, however resulted in a time of remarkable flourishing in the life of the church during his pastorate and that of his successor. The membership of the church dramatically increased during this period as Castle baptized some 537 professing believers during his Toronto ministry.[135] Castle

---

[133] "Jarvis Street Baptist Church Minute Book 1866–1881," Minutes of December 18, 1872, and December 23, 1872.
[134] B.D. Thomas, "The Beginning Growth of Baptist Interests in Toronto" (Handwritten ms., McMaster Divinity College Archives, McMaster University, Hamilton, Ontario).
[135] *A Citadel of Truth for a Century. Centennial Banquet Dec. 2, 1975* ([Toronto: Jarvis Street Baptist Church,] 1975), 17. This booklet is in the Jarvis Street Baptist Church Archives, Toronto, ON.

also played a central role in the establishment in 1879 of what would be initially called Toronto Baptist College, and which would go on to become known as McMaster University. And, most significantly with regard to the future, three years earlier he had led the church in a building programme that eventuated in an impressive new church building for the congregation on the corner of Jarvis and Gerrard Streets.

Toronto Baptist College/McMaster University

When Robert Alexander Fyfe died in 1878, a number of Ontario Baptists, including Castle as well as William and Susan McMaster, raised the idea of re-locating the theological department of the Canadian Literary Institute to Toronto, a bustling city of 90,000 people at the time with eleven Baptist churches and mission stations.[136] They were anxious to have a distinctive and influential Baptist voice in the political and economic centre of the province. Fyfe had long argued for a better-educated Baptist ministry to raise denominational respectability.[137] It is not surprising that some of his fellow Baptists like the McMasters and a goodly number of upwardly mobile businessmen also wanted to couple this with a growing influence in the public sector of society. John Castle and William McMaster skilfully argued for the move to Toronto, even though this would entail the dismemberment of the Canadian Literary Institute in Woodstock.[138] At a lengthy meeting of the denominational leadership in First Baptist Church, Guelph, on July 17, 1879, Castle, McMaster and their friends carried the day and it was decided to move the theology department of the Canadian Literary Institute from Woodstock to Toronto. McMaster donated the site on Bloor Street for

---

[136] See also Holman, "Susan Moulton McMaster," 145.
[137] Daniel C. Goodwin, " 'The Footprints of Zion's King': Baptists in Canada to 1880" in G.A. Rawlyk, ed., *Aspects of the Canadian Evangelical Experience* (Montreal, QC; Kingston, ON: McGill-Queen's University Press, 1997), 201.
[138] Johnston, "Castle, John Harvard." On the key role also played by Susan Moulton McMaster in supporting her husband's vision, see Thomson, "William McMaster," 99–100.

what was to be called the Toronto Baptist College.[139] He also gave an initial $100,000 to the cause and pledged an additional sum of $14,500 annually. Construction was finished in the summer of 1881, and that fall classes began. As McMaster once said:

> ...the Baptists are a peculiar people; they cannot train their sons for the ministry from their childhood as a profession, because they do not believe in anyone entering that holy calling without his being chosen of God, and now, as always, God seems to choose chiefly from the ranks of the poor. If we are to have a properly equipped ministry this makes our obligation greater than those of other denominations.[140]

The theological statement of the new school contained a strong affirmation of both Calvinism and closed communion. "The election and effectual calling of all God's people" was affirmed, along with "the atoning efficacy of the Death of Christ, the free justification of believers in Him by his imputed righteousness" and "the preservation unto eternal life of the Saints." "Immersion in the name of the Father the Son and the Holy Spirit" was confessed to be the "only gospel 'baptism'." And only those "so baptized are ... entitled to Communion at the Lord's Table."[141] It is a statement that is fully in line with the doctrinal position of most Ontario Baptists of the nineteenth century.[142]

Up until his death in 1887, McMaster dreamed of moving the rest of the Woodstock Institute to Toronto and establishing a first-class university. Driven by a great desire to establish a major Baptist

---

[139] The name chosen for the school was McMaster's suggestion. There were some who wanted to name the theological college after McMaster, but, while he was alive, he would not hear of it. He did acquiesce to the use of the term "McMaster Hall" for the name of the building, however. See Thomson, "William McMaster," 100–101.

[140] Cited Thomson, "William McMaster," 99.

[141] Cited G.A. Rawlyk, "A.L. McCrimmon, H.P. Whidden, T.T. Shields, Christian Higher Education, and McMaster University" in his ed., *Canadian Baptists and Christian Higher Education* (Kingston, ON; Montreal, QC: McGill-Queen's University Press, 1988), 32–33. See Appendix 2 for the full statement of faith.

[142] See the overall argument of William Norman Albert Gillespie, "Ontario's 19th Century Baptist Tradition: Its Roots and its Development" (PhD thesis, University of Waterloo, 1990).

presence in the heart of the most influential city in Ontario and to demonstrate that Baptists were as respectable as other denominational bodies, he worked towards this goal, which was finally achieved in the year of his death. To secure the dream he left a $900,000 bequest in his will to the new school, which was an enormous sum of money.[143] The school would be appropriately named McMaster University after his death. The university was designed to be a Christian institution of higher learning, though only the seminary was to be explicitly Baptist.[144]

---

[143] Johnston, Cameron, *et al.*, "McMaster, William."
[144] Rawlyk, "A.L. McCrimmon, H.P. Whidden, T.T. Shields," 40–41.

McMaster University in Toronto

7

Jarvis Street Baptist Church and Toronto Baptist College

♦ ♦ ♦

BEFORE TORONTO BAPTIST COLLEGE began its classes in the fall of 1881, John Castle was asked to teach in systematic and pastoral theology as well as to become the school's president. Castle accepted and this necessitated his resignation from the pastorate of Jarvis Street in April of 1881.[145] In an April 16 letter to the congregation, the Board of Trustees of the college stressed that their calling Castle to be president had been reached after "much prayer and careful consideration." The trustees were confident that the choice of Castle as president would be greeted with universal approbation by Baptists in both Canada and the United States.[146] In their response to this turn of events, the Jarvis Street members recognized the will of God at work and wrote to the trustees that

> as the law of Christ is not to seek our own welfare only but that of others, they feel constrained to consent to your desire to let him enter your service. They do so the more cheerfully from the consideration that although to be an under shepherd over a portion of Christ's flock is a highly useful and honourable position, yet the one to which you have assigned him is still more useful, honourable and important than of teaching and training those who under the Great Shepherd are to become the Leaders of God's people. A teacher of the people is a responsible office, a teacher of teachers more so.[147]

---

[145] "Jarvis Street Baptist Church Minute Book 1866–1881," Minute of April 22, 1881 (Jarvis Street Baptist Church Archives, Toronto, ON).

[146] This letter was copied into the "Jarvis Street Baptist Church Minute Book 1866–1881," Minute of April 22, 1881.

[147] "Jarvis Street Baptist Church Minute Book 1866–1881," Minute of April 22, 1881. Two commas have been added.

Subsequently Castle sought, along with the other faculty, to train Baptist pastors for two worlds: rural Ontario as well as the growing urban industrial centers like Toronto and Hamilton at the head of Lake Ontario. But the school's location on Bloor Street placed the Baptist school right next to the University of Toronto and there was pressure in the early years to federate with this University as the Methodist Victoria College and the Anglican Trinity College had done in 1890 and 1904 respectively. It was Castle who argued against this path as he sought to preserve McMaster as an independent university under the auspices of the Ontario and Quebec Baptists.[148]

The other key legacy of John Castle's ministry was the move of the congregation from Bond Street to Jarvis Street, and here again McMaster played a key role as benefactor.

Building on "a most desirable site"

It was not long after Castle came to the pastorate at Bond Street that he realized that the church building was too small to accommodate the growing numbers of worshippers at the church. By mid-April of 1873—less than four months after Castle had agreed to come to Toronto to pastor the Bond Street work—a building committee, which included William McMaster, had been struck "to consider and report on the advisability of the erection of the new church edifice."[149] By June $30,000 had been raised to cover the actual costs of the building, exclusive of the site, and *The Canadian Baptist*, reporting on this venture, congratulated the Bond Street Church members on their "devising liberal things."[150] It took a while to find a site, though. Finally, at the beginning of 1874, McMaster reported back to the church that the building committee had found "a most desirable site"

---

[148] Charles M. Johnston, "Castle, John Harvard," *Dictionary of Canadian Biography*, 11 (University of Toronto; Université Laval, 2003–2018; http://www.biographi.ca/en/bio/castle_john_harvard_11E.html; accessed May 2, 2023).

[149] "Jarvis Street Baptist Church Minute Book 1866–1881," Minute of April 14, 1873.

[150] "Bond St. Church, Toronto," *The Canadian Baptist* 19, no.21 (June 19, 1873). See also "Jarvis Street Baptist Church Minute Book 1866–1881," Minute of June 18, 1873.

for the new church building at the north-east corner of Jarvis and Gerrard Streets that could "be obtained for the very reasonable sum of $8,500." The church unanimously approved the purchase of the lot, which, as it turned out, was totally paid for by the McMasters.[151] Four days later the sale was completed and McMaster, along with four others, were appointed trustees of what the Minute Book called "Jarvis Street Regular Baptist Church."[152]

It is also noteworthy that Edmund Burke (1850–1919), one of the church's deacons and also a rising star in the world of Canadian architecture, was added to the building committee at this point.[153] Born in Toronto, the eldest son of the lumber merchant and builder William Burke, Edmund was apprenticed to his architect uncle Henry Langley (1836–1907) at the age of 14 after he had finished his school education at Upper Canada College. In the course of his career Langley designed no fewer than 70 church buildings across Ontario for virtually every major denomination, making him the most prolific church architect of nineteenth-century Ontario.[154] Most of his church buildings exhibit the style known as Gothic Revival. This form of architecture, which looked to medieval cathedrals for inspiration, was initially linked with the Anglo-Catholic revival of the 1820s and 1830s that sought to reinvigorate Christianity by a return to pre-Reformation practices and piety. Gothic Revival architects used soaring spires, great

---

[151] "Jarvis Street Baptist Church Minute Book 1866–1881," Minute of January 26, 1874.

[152] "Jarvis Street Baptist Church Minute Book 1866–1881," Minute of January 26, 1874. On the change of name, see also "Jarvis Street Baptist Church Minute Book 1866–1881," Minute of December 21, 1875.

[153] "Jarvis Street Baptist Church Minute Book 1866–1881," Minute of January 26, 1874. For the life and career of Burke, see especially Angela Carr, *Toronto Architect Edmund Burke: Redefining Canadian Architecture* (Montreal, QC; Kingston, ON: McGill-Queen's University Press, 1995). For a brief overview of his career, see Angela Carr, "Burke, Edmund (1850–1919)" in *Dictionary of Canadian Biography*, vol. 14 (University of Toronto/Université Laval, 2003–) (http://www.biographi.ca/en/bio/burke_edmund_1850_1919_14E.html; accessed May 3, 2023).

[154] Candace Iron, "Henry Langley's Catholic Church Commissions: Adapting Charles Borromeo's *Instructiones* to the Gothic Revival in Canada," *Journal of the Society for the Study of Architecture in Canada* 38, no. 1 (2013): 47.

naves and stained glass to promote their religious convictions. By the 1870s, though, Evangelical Protestant churches in both Britain and Canada were also employing Gothic Revival architecture for their churches. Of course, these churches did not endorse Anglo-Catholic theology, let alone Roman Catholic thinking. They were simply using Gothic Revival architectural forms for decorative and aesthetic purposes. Yet, as architectural historian Gilbert Stelter has noted, even this superficial use of the Gothic style would have been considered unacceptable to Evangelical churches twenty or thirty years earlier, for Gothic Revival architecture was closely associated with both Anglo-Catholicism and Roman Catholicism.[155]

Burke was thus trained under the tutelage of one of the finest Gothic Revival architects, but right from the beginning of his architectural career he demonstrated an innovative streak. Burke entered into a formal partnership with his uncle in 1873. His first important and independent commission was Jarvis Street Baptist Church, which was built with costly Queenston stone and totally paid for by the McMasters.[156] Here he reveals the influence of his mentor Langley in the Gothic Revival exterior, even down to the use of gargoyles. But the interior is quite innovative. Burke arranged the seating as an amphitheatre, the first like it in Toronto and possibly even Canada. This design had roots in the meeting-houses of New England as well as the urban theatres used by American itinerant evangelists for evangelistic meetings.[157] Its effect on worshippers is well captured by the words of one visitor to the church in 1895: "Entering the church, you find it spacious and comfortable, quietly and tastefully decorated, and pleasant and restful to the eye. There is an unmistakable home-like feeling about it."[158] Up to thirteen hundred or so could easily meet for worship seated in the pews in the main

---

[155] Gilbert A. Stelter, "Henry Langley and the Making of Gothic Guelph," *Historic Guelph*, 28 (September 1989): 4–30, *passim*. See also Carr, *Toronto Architect Edmund Burke*, 25.
[156] Carr, *Toronto Architect Edmund Burke*, 26–27.
[157] Carr, *Toronto Architect Edmund Burke*, 27–29.
[158] J. R. N., "Pew and Pulpit in Toronto.—VII. At Jarvis Street Baptist Church," *The Week* 12, no.9 (April 5, 1895): 439.

auditorium of the church and its gallery. If extra chairs were added another seven hundred could be accommodated.

The final sermon at Bond Street was preached on November 28, 1875, by R. A. Fyfe, who was especially invited back to deliver the talk, "A Forty Years' Survey from Bond St. Pulpit."[159] In the evening, the service lasted more than three hours as both current and previous members shared about what God was doing in their lives.[160] The following Thursday the congregation met at their new church location for a formal dedication of the building. Castle had asked the man under whom he had been converted, J. Lansing Burrows, to come from Louisville, Kentucky, to preach. Burrows spoke in the afternoon at 2:00 p.m. from Psalm 45:15 ("With gladness and rejoicing shall they be brought: they shall enter into the king's palace," KJV). He noted that in the King's palace, "no pope or prelate, no priest nor presbytery, no conference nor council has a right to legislate." Only the King can exercise authority there, for "each Church is a chosen company called out from the world and separated from it, for his service and glory, in absolute submission to his authority and in unquestioning obedience to his laws." This is classic Baptist polity. Burrows closed with a dedicatory prayer:

> To the one living and true God, Father, Son, and Holy Ghost, do we now devoutly, heartily, joyfully consecrate this building—this pulpit ... these pews ... this choir ... this baptistery ... this whole building we declare set apart and devoted to the service and worship of God and to the spiritual culture and guidance of men. Holy Father! Blessed Redeemer! Gracious Spirit! Accept the offering we now freely make, and here display Thy glory, exert Thy power, manifest Thy love, convert sinners, edify Thy saints, discipline Thy Church for usefulness on earth and for rest

---

[159] "Jarvis Street Baptist Church Minute Book 1866–1881," Minute of November 28, 1874. This sermon would eventually be published by Fyfe as *A Forty Years' Survey From Bond Street Pulpit* (Toronto, ON: Dudley & Burns, 1876).
[160] "Jarvis Street Baptist Church Minute Book 1866–1881," Minute of November 28, 1874.

in heaven, and Thine shall be the praise, through Jesus Christ our Lord.[161]

The following Lord's Day evening, December 5, 1875, Burrows preached again to a congregation of some two thousand people. It was reckoned that another thousand were turned away. Castle had asked Burrows to preach to the unconverted in the audience from Isaiah 52:1 ("Awake, awake; put on thy strength, O Zion; put on thy beautiful garments, O Jerusalem," KJV). A later report described the sermon as "one of the most effective and solemn" the reporter had ever heard and that Burrows was "the impersonation of sacred eloquence."[162]

Five years and four months later, Castle left the Jarvis Street church to become the president of Toronto Baptist College. Though his pastorate at Jarvis Street had been only a little more than eight years, he had led the church in a significant building program on Jarvis Street that has obviously shaped the life and worship of the congregation down to the present day. He was also a key player in the formation of what became McMaster University, an important Baptist institution. He did not live to see the flourishing of this university as ill-health led to his retirement in 1889 and his return to the United States, where he died two years later. Ironically thirty-five years after Castle's death the clash of these two legacies of Castle—the Jarvis Street congregation and McMaster University—would also be a central element in what these two institutions became in the twentieth century.

---

[161] "The Baptist Pulpit. Brought into the King's Palace," *The Canadian Baptist* 21, no.49 (December 9, 1875): 1. See also "Jarvis Street Baptist Church Minute Book 1866–1881," Minute of December 2, 1875.

[162] "Dedication of Jarvis Street Church," *The Canadian Baptist* 21, no.49 (December 9, 1875).

Benjamin Daniel Thomas

8

A Welsh Baptist: Benjamin Daniel Thomas

♦ ♦ ♦

IT WAS IN September of 1868 that the congregation of Tabernacle English Baptist Church that met for worship on Water Street in Neath, Glamorganshire, said farewell to their minister Benjamin Daniel Thomas, who had served the congregation, his first pastorate, for the previous six years.[163] With his wife and children, he had decided to leave Wales and emigrate to Pennsylvania in the United States. The *Swansea Herald* reported details of the official farewell, at which a gift of appreciation, a purse of £30, was given to Rev. Thomas and heartfelt thanks expressed for his ministry.[164] But what was not reported

---

[163] For the biographical details of Thomas' life I am indebted to the following: William Cathcart, *The Baptist Encyclopaedia* (Philadelphia, PA: Louis H. Everts, 1881), 1147 (along with this brief biographical sketch there is also a portrait of Thomas in his late thirties); "Thomas, Benjamin Daniel" in George Maclean Rose, *A Cyclopaedia of Canadian Biography: Being Chiefly Men of the Time* (Toronto, ON: Rose Publishing Co., 1888), 379–380; "Thomas, Rev. Benjamin Daniel" in Henry James Morgan, ed., *The Canadian Men and Women of the Time: A Hand-book of Canadian Biography* (Toronto, ON: William Briggs, 1898), 1005; "Thomas, Rev. Benjamin Daniel" in Henry James Morgan, ed., *The Canadian Men and Women of the Time: A Hand-book of Canadian Biography of Living Characters*, 2nd ed. (Toronto, ON: William Briggs, 1912), 1093; F. Tracy, "In Memoriam Dr. B.D. Thomas," *The Canadian Baptist* 89, no.4 (February 15, 1943). 2.

Besides the portrait noted above in Cathcart's *Baptist Encyclopaedia*, there are also a couple of photographs in the McMaster Divinity College Archives, one of which is from 1891–1892, the year that Thomas served as the President of the Baptist Convention of Ontario and Quebec. There is also a photograph taken when Thomas was around sixty and that appears as the frontispiece to his *The Secret of Divine Silence*.

[164] "Testimonial to a Neath Baptist Minister" ([Newspaper clipping in an envelope in B.D. Thomas, "My Pastorate in Toronto" [Scrapbook of newspaper

was why he and his wife, Mary, née Jones (d.1886),[165] were leaving Wales.

During the seventeenth and eighteenth centuries numbers of Thomas' Baptist forbears had also left Wales. Men like John Miles (1621–1683), who had founded a Baptist work at Ilston, near Swansea, in 1649, felt they had no option but to emigrate to New England in 1663 owing to persecution from state authorities.[166] Miles was typical of that era of emigration from Wales, in which Welsh emigrants, many of them Baptists, moved to America for religious freedom.[167] By the nineteenth century, though, Welsh emigration westwards was largely owing to economic reasons. Economic depression and social distress in the 1820s and 1830s following the Napoleonic Wars made American land, business opportunities, and social egalitarianism quite attractive to a good number of the Welsh, although Welsh emigration never matched that from other parts of Great Britain, especially Ireland. The population sizes of Wales and Ireland during this era were not too different, but the Irish emigrated in their millions while the Welsh left Wales only in tens of thousands.[168] One key reason for this

---

clippings, McMaster Divinity College Archives, McMaster University, Hamilton, ON]). Thomas commenced this scrapbook of newspaper cuttings about his ministry, his sermons, and Jarvis Street Baptist Church when he came to Toronto in the autumn of 1882, but it also contains items from earlier phases of his ministry.

[165] "Thomas, Rev. Benjamin Daniel" in Morgan, ed., *Canadian Men and Women of the Time* (1898), 1005.

[166] Alan Conway, "Welsh Emigration to the United States," *Perspectives in American History* 7 (1973): 184–185. The following observations about Welsh emigration are indebted to this article which remains the best study of Welsh emigration to the United States. On Miles, see also Thomas Richards, "Miles, John" in R.T. Jenkins, ed., *The Dictionary of Welsh Biography Down to 1940* (London: The Honourable Society of Cymmrodorion, 1959), 632–633; T.M. Bassett, *The Welsh Baptists* (Swansea: Ilston House, 1977), 13–41, *passim*; B.R. White, "John Miles and the Structures of the Calvinistic Baptist Mission to South Wales 1649–1660" in *Welsh Baptist Studies*, ed. Mansel John ([Cardiff]: South Wales Baptist College, 1976), 35–76.

[167] Conway, "Welsh Emigration," 183–191, 266–267.

[168] Conway, "Welsh Emigration," 191–271. According to American immigration figures, some ninety thousand Welsh left Wales for America between 1820 and 1950. This figure, though, is significantly less than the actual numbers since many

A WELSH BAPTIST: BENJAMIN DANIEL THOMAS

difference in numbers of emigrants was the mid-nineteenth-century development of South Wales into one of the world's leading industrial centres.[169]

What is almost certain, though, about Thomas' decision to emigrate is that such a momentous decision would not have been taken without prayer, for uppermost with him as a Christian was obedience to the Lord Christ and doing his Master's will. As he stated in a sermon on 1 Thessalonians 5:16–18, "the determinative quality in all true prayer is acquiescence in the divine will."[170]

"The supreme aim of the gospel ministry"

Benjamin Daniel Thomas had been raised in a pastor's home. His father, Benjamin Thomas (1792–1862), was the third pastor of Bethesda Baptist Church, Narberth, Pembrokeshire. The senior Thomas had been called to this church in 1823 after studying under William Steadman (1764–1837) in the Horton Academy at Bradford, Yorkshire, and had faithfully pastored the Pembrokeshire cause for the next thirty-nine years.[171] The younger Thomas had moved away from home during his early teens to study at Graig House Academy, a grammar school in Swansea,[172] for four years before going to Haverfordwest Baptist College, which had been founded in the late 1830s.[173] Here, under the principalship of Thomas Davies (1812–

---

of the Welsh emigrants appear to have been classified as English. See Conway, "Welsh Emigration," 191–192.

[169] Conway, "Welsh Emigration," 227.

[170] B.D. Thomas, "The Habitual Temper of the Christian Life" in his *The Secret of Divine Silence and Other Sermons* (Toronto, ON: William Briggs, 1903), 213. This book of sermons was re-published eight years later as *Sermons: Preached in the Jarvis Street Baptist Church, Toronto* (Toronto, ON: William Briggs, 1911).

[171] For a history of this church, see W.H.Williams, "History of Bethesda, Narberth" in *Bethesda Baptist Church, Narberth, 1808–1958* (Narberth, Pembrokeshire: H.G. Walters, 1958), 13–20. In the Canadian Baptist Archives at McMaster Divinity College, there is a ms. book of the senior Thomas' sermons.

[172] This grammar school was run by a Baptist minister George Pritchard Evans (1820–1874), a graduate of Bristol Baptist Academy and one time missionary to Jamaica. He ran the Swansea grammar school, which educated numerous ministers, from 1846 till his death. See William Joseph Rhys, "Evans, George Pritchard" in *Dictionary of Welsh Biography*, 235.

[173] Bassett, *Welsh Baptists*, 196–197.

1895), who also served as the pastor of Bethesda Baptist Church at Haverfordwest,[174] he pursued a regular programme of theological study and appears to have graduated in 1861, the year that he was ordained.

As noted above, his first pastoral charge was at Neath, where he went in 1862 when he was but nineteen. Two years later he married Mary Jones. The couple had six children, one of whom, Llewellyn Thomas, followed in his father's and grandfather's footsteps and became a preacher of the gospel. Their marriage, though, was a brief eighteen years, for Mary died in 1886 in Toronto.

When Thomas and his family emigrated to America in the autumn of 1868, they went first to Pittston in Pennsylvania—this state being a favourite locale for many Welsh emigrants. There he pastored the Baptist Church for three years, from 1868 to 1871. He then moved to the Fifth Baptist Church, Philadelphia, one of the largest Baptist works in that part of the state, where he served for eleven years. A defining mark of his ministry during this period was evangelistic preaching that made a point of seeking the conversion of unbelievers. As he said in a sermon that he first preached around 1878:

> A church (I care not what her wealth or influence or numbers) is a failure unless souls are born in her, unless she walks the earth, so to speak, under the profound impulse of a divine unction and in the enthusiasm of conscious power, unless she can ... quicken dead souls into an immortal being by the supernatural energies of her God-given life. This is her glory and her praise ...[175]

This meant that the salvation of the lost, Thomas continued, should be "the supreme aim of the gospel ministry":

> To prostitute the pulpit to any other end than this, to make it the Thermopylae for intellectual display or rhetorical effect, to use it for mercenary or ambitious designs, or to employ it as an

---

[174] On Davies, see Benjamin George Owens, "Davies, Thomas" in *Dictionary of Welsh Biography*, 154.

[175] "The Glory of the Church" in Thomas, *The Secret of Divine Silence*, 81–82. For another example of a sermon he preached during his Philadelphia pastorate, see *Memorial Sermon on William Mann, of Philadelphia* ([Philadelphia, PA, 1881]).

arena for personal exhibition, must be an impertinence for which a parallel could scarcely be produced. To have no higher aim in our ministrations than to gratify and amuse, or to seek to have the interest of our audiences culminate in admiration of ourselves, is an exhibition at which angels might well weep. … The one dominating, controlling, all-subduing purpose of the ministerial life should be the salvation of souls. This should be ever nearest to our hearts and foremost in our lives.[176]

Not surprisingly, other North American Baptist churches that were without pastors began to consider calling a preacher with this kind of evangelistic emphasis in his pulpit ministry. One such church was Jarvis Street Baptist Church in Toronto, where the type of evangelistic emphasis that marked Thomas' preaching was highly prized.[177]

"The hand of the Lord"

As noted in the previous chapter, John Castle stepped down from the pastorate of Jarvis Street in 1880 when he assumed the Presidency of Toronto Baptist College. Castle had come to Toronto from Philadelphia and it may well have been through his acquaintance with the Baptist causes in Philadelphia that Thomas was asked to fill the pulpit for two July Sundays in 1882.[178] Immediately after the service on the second Sunday, July 23, a special meeting was convened to consider extending a call to Thomas to be the pastor of the church.

---

[176] "The Glory of the Church" in Thomas, *The Secret of Divine Silence*, 82–83. See also Thomas' remarks about a close friend, the Welsh preacher Frederick Evans (1840–1897): "The preaching that had no divine sacrifice for sin to announce, no almighty Saviour to proclaim, no perfected righteousness to offer, no eternal life to invite to, he from his very heart despised"—and, it might be added, so did Thomas (*Frederick Evans, D.D. (Ednyfed). A Memorial*, ed. B.D. Thomas [Philadelphia, PA: American Baptist Publication Society, 1899], 101). On Evans, see also David Emrys Evans, "Evans, Frederick" in *Dictionary of Welsh Biography*, 234.

[177] For a brief history of this church, see Glenn V. Tomlinson and Andrew M. Fountain, ed., *"From Strength to Strength": A Pictorial History Of Jarvis Street Baptist Church 1818–1993* (Toronto, ON: Gospel Witness Publications, 1993). See also n. 112. above.

[178] "Minutes of the Jarvis Street Baptist Church, Toronto, Ontario, April 24, 1881–April 20, 1892" (Jarvis Street Baptist Church, Toronto, Ontario), Minutes of July 16 and 23, 1882.

JESUS, WONDROUS SAVIOUR

The members at this meeting voted unanimously to call Thomas, who sent an acceptance letter on August 9.[179] Thomas told the Toronto Baptists that making the decision to relocate to Canada was "one of the most painful ordeals" he had ever experienced. He found it extremely difficult to contemplate leaving those whom he had come to love in his Philadelphia pastorate, who had been so kind to him and who were, he said, "most earnest and united" in their not wanting him to leave them. "If it were not for the conviction which has fastened itself upon my mind, that the hand of the Lord is in it," Thomas continued, he most definitely would have declined. But his heart's desire was to submit to the Lord's leadership and have his "steps so ordered that the largest Glory may result to His great name."[180]

If Thomas had doubts about the rightness of relocating to Toronto, the blessing attending his ministry at Jarvis Street would have dispelled those doubts. During Thomas' pastorate, the average Sunday morning worship attendance was around nine hundred with twelve to fifteen hundred filling the auditorium for the evening service.[181] In our next chapter, we shall consider some details of that Toronto ministry.

---

[179] "Minutes of the Jarvis Street Baptist Church," Minutes of July 23, 1882; August 13, 1882 (the letter was dated August 9, 1882). There is also an extant telegram dated August 9, 1882, sent from Ocean Beach, New Jersey, that indicated that this letter was on its way (McMaster Divinity College Archives, McMaster University, Hamilton, Ontario).

[180] Letter to Jarvis Street Baptist Church, August 9, 1882 in "Minutes of the Jarvis Street Baptist Church," Minute of August 13, 1882.

[181] [J. Ross Robertson,] *Sketches in City Churches* (Toronto, ON: J. Ross Robertson, 1886), 26.

Jarvis Street Baptist Church

9

"Dr. Thomas of Toronto"

◆ ◆ ◆

B.D. THOMAS officially began his ministry at Jarvis Street on the second Sunday in October 1882,[182] and the following month, he and his wife, as well two of their daughters—Gertie and Millie, who had been baptized as believers in Philadelphia—were received into the membership of the Jarvis Street congregation.[183] There was also a special service of induction held at which a number of the key Toronto Baptist leaders of the day, including John Castle, Joshua Denovan (1829–1901), and E.W. Dadson (1845–1900), took part.[184] A newspaper report that Thomas preserved of his induction as pastor mentioned that the welcome accorded to Thomas by "the members of

---

[182] Newspaper clipping in B.D. Thomas, "My Pastorate in Toronto" (Scrapbook of newspaper clippings, McMaster Divinity College Archives, McMaster University, Hamilton, ON); *Souvenir of the Tenth Anniversary of the Settlement of Rev. B.D. Thomas with the Jarvis Street Baptist Church* (Toronto, ON: Davis & Henderson, 1892), 9.

[183] "Minutes of the Jarvis Street Baptist Church," Minute of November 5, 1882.

[184] On Denovan, see O.C.S. Wallace et al., *Joshua Denovan* (Toronto, ON: Standard Publ. Co., 1901); on Dadson, see Jones H. Farmer, ed., *E.W. Dadson, B.A., D.D., the man and his message* (Toronto, ON: William Briggs, 1902). Thomas preached a funeral sermon for Dadson from 1 Timothy 4:6 and gave a tribute to Denovan based on Romans 1:1. See the newspaper clippings in Thomas, "My Pastorate in Toronto."

When Denovan was living, Thomas said of him in the 1880s: he "is a man of unusual intellectual force … If he were not so exclusive in his habits and Samsonic in the exercise of his strength, he would be a felt power in all this land. We may not always accept his dictum, but he never speaks nor writes but what he stirs every sluggish fibre of our being" ("From Toronto" [Newspaper clipping in Thomas, "My Pastorate in Toronto"]).

his flock and Baptists of Toronto was enthusiastic in the extreme," with some twelve hundred present for the occasion.[185]

When Thomas came to the Toronto church he soon realized that the membership roll, which stood at 718, was somewhat inflated. Through careful revision a more accurate number of 612 was reached.[186] Over the next ten years, 950 were received into the church—432 through conversion and baptism and 518 by letters of dismission from other churches. At the same time, though, 727 had either left or died, giving a net gain of 223 over the decade.[187] During his second decade of ministry, another 695 joined the church, 288 by baptism after conversion and 407 by dismissal from another Baptist cause. When Thomas resigned the pastoral charge of the church in the summer of 1903, the membership stood at 896.[188] What is noteworthy is that during his pastorate the numbers attending the mid-week prayer-meeting averaged between 400 and 500, something that was considered remarkable even in that day of large congregations.[189]

All of this growth came at a time when people were beginning to move out of the inner city where the church was located for what were then the suburbs. And although Thomas himself distrusted statistics—the "summing up of the results of spiritual activity by an imposing array of figures has always appeared to me," he said on one occasion, "a vain-glorious exhibition"[190]—these figures do indicate that his ministry was powerfully owned by God for the conversion and blessing of many in Toronto during the final two decades of the nineteenth century.

---

[185] Newspaper clipping in Thomas, "My Pastorate in Toronto."
[186] *Souvenir of the Tenth Anniversary*, 9.
[187] *Souvenir of the Tenth Anniversary*, 9–10.
[188] "Rev. Dr. Thomas Resigns" (Newspaper clipping in Thomas, "My Pastorate in Toronto").
[189] [J. Ross Robertson,] *Sketches in City Churches* (Toronto, ON: J. Ross Robertson, 1886), 28; "Rev. Dr. Thomas" (Newspaper clipping in Thomas, "My Pastorate in Toronto"). The latter also describes Thomas' public prayers at the prayer-meeting: "poems of adoration, thankfulness and desire for uplifting into better life and more pious impulse … the Psalmist seems to be his model."
[190] *Souvenir of the Tenth Anniversary*, 9.

"Dr. THOMAS OF TORONTO"

One final point that needs to be stressed about Thomas was that although he came to love Canada,[191] he never lost his love for Wales, returning there a number of times for vacation during his Toronto pastorate.[192] As he said one occasion, after one such vacation in Wales:

> For miniature scenes of natural loveliness, for narrow mountain gorges, for romantic glens nestling at the base of wild and rugged steeps, for beautiful streams breaking here and there into cascades and waterfalls, and for a simplicity of life beautified with a religious quality, Wales is unsurpassed.[193]

On these visits to Wales, Thomas usually spent several weeks at Narberth where he preached in the church his father had pastored and came to be known as "Dr. Thomas of Toronto."[194] In fact, so enamoured was Thomas of his Welsh heritage that on one occasion as he was reflecting on the beauty of the Welsh language he stated that it was "destined to be spoken in the new Eden to which we all look forward with fervent expectation"![195]

"To be a preacher"

Thomas was also convinced—and this on much surer grounds than his linguistic expectations—that if Wales

---

[191] See, for example, his report about enjoying winter sports in Montreal, "From Toronto" (Newspaper clipping in Thomas, "My Pastorate in Toronto").

[192] For example, he was in Wales for vacation from June to August, 1885, the year before the death of his wife. See "Minutes of the Jarvis Street Baptist Church," Minute of April 24, 1885, where the membership of the church gave their "cordial approval" to Thomas' request to go to Wales for "the purpose of visiting friends" over a period of "two or three months." He went there again in the summer of 1896; see "Vacation Experiences" (Newspaper clipping in Thomas, "My Pastorate in Toronto"). See also his account of a vacation to Wales and the European Continent that he took in the company of his close friend Frederick Evans: *Frederick Evans, D.D. (Ednyfed). A Memorial*, ed. B.D. Thomas (Philadelphia, PA: American Baptist Publication Society, 1899), 137–138.

[193] "Vacation Experiences" (Newspaper clipping in Thomas, "My Pastorate in Toronto").

[194] W.H. Williams, "History of Bethesda, Narberth" in *Bethesda Baptist Church, Narberth, 1808–1958* (Narberth, Pembrokeshire: H.G. Walters, 1958), 16.

[195] "Vacation Experiences" (Newspaper clipping in Thomas, "My Pastorate in Toronto").

> has not produced statesmen and artists, philosophers and scholars, who could stand without suggestion of inferiority beside the best product of other lands, she has produced preachers who certainly could. What philosophers were in Greece, and artists in Italy, preachers have been and still continue to be in Wales, the consummate blossoming of her richest life.
>
> ... it is but natural that the pulpit should strongly appeal to the imagination of the youth of the principality when brought under the regenerating influence of God's Holy Spirit. To be a preacher, to the Welsh lad of fifty years ago [i.e., the 1840s] was a greater object of aspiration than to be aught else beneath the sun.[196]

The final remarks probably well reflect Thomas' own desires after he was converted, for there is good evidence that he began to preach in his teens.

By the time Thomas came to Toronto he was at the height of his powers as a preacher. One of those who heard him at this time likened him to a prophet, a man "with a message" and noted that "to listen to Dr. Thomas is to be reminded of the orthodoxy of thirty or forty years ago," that is, the 1840s, before the advent of Higher Criticism that brought many to doubt the veracity of God's Word.[197] Another called

---

[196] Thomas, ed., *Frederick Evans, D.D.*, 92, 95. For similar words, see "Vacation Experiences" (Newspaper clipping in Thomas, "My Pastorate in Toronto").

In an address entitled "The Welshman as a Factor in American History," Thomas noted that the Welsh emigrants brought to America "a quality of being that had been disciplined in virtue, that had been nurtured in the love of liberty and righteousness, that had a supreme reverence for God, that had an intelligent apprehension of the teaching of the Bible, that had an ardent zeal for all that tended to the moral, intellectual and spiritual well-being of the race. They became, wherever they chanced to take up their abode, centres of influence that acted with a beneficent and healthful potency upon the formative elements that were then determining the complexion of the nation's life. They did not figure as prominently as the representatives of other lands in material, social or political enterprises, but they gave to the country of their adoption impulses toward higher living and moral and spiritual attainment, which it would be altogether impossible to estimate." (Newspaper clipping in Thomas, "My Pastorate in Toronto").

[197] J.R.N., "Pew and Pulpit in Toronto.—VII. At Jarvis Street Baptist Church," *The Week* 12, no.19 (April 5, 1895): 439.

"Dr. THOMAS OF TORONTO"

him a "most powerful and eloquent preacher."[198] In contrast to other popular preachers of the Victorian era, though, Thomas was not considered an orator by those who heard him, for his preaching style tended to be free from the sort of ornamentation favoured by many in his day.[199] Moreover, Thomas was careful not to play on the emotions of his hearers,[200] although one critic felt that he needed to be more direct in his preaching and point out how men and women are "seriously deformed by sin."[201] After Thomas' death, it was noted that he was not fond of controversy,[202] yet, there is good evidence, as shall be seen below, that Thomas was not hesitant in proclaiming all of God's truth as found in his Word. In Thomas' opinion, it was vital for Christians to be deeply committed to the Scriptures and the whole of their truth, for they were living in a day

> when nothing appears to be established, when transitions and transformations, the most rapid and amazing, are taking place around us. The swirling waters of intellectual speculation are casting up the deposits of centuries. The very foundations of belief are undermined ... There are those who assure us that we have been deluded; that the citadel of our faith is a poor, tawdry fabric, reared by superstition and ignorance; that the highest truths in which we have sought comfort and inspiration are without foundation; that is nothing is absolutely certain that is not open to scientific or mathematical demonstration.[203]

---

[198] "Thomas, Rev. Benjamin Daniel" in Henry James Morgan, ed., *The Canadian Men and Women of the Time: A Hand-book of Canadian Biography of Living Characters*, 2nd ed. (Toronto, ON: William Briggs, 1912), 1093.

[199] [Robertson,] *Sketches in City Churches*, 31; J.R.N., "Pew and Pulpit in Toronto.—VII. At Jarvis Street Baptist Church," 439–440.

[200] "Rev. Dr. Thomas" (Newspaper clipping in Thomas, "My Pastorate in Toronto").

[201] "Rev. Dr. Thomas" (Newspaper clipping in Thomas, "My Pastorate in Toronto").

[202] F. Tracy, "In Memoriam Dr. B.D. Thomas," *The Canadian Baptist* 89, no.4 (February 15, 1943): 2.

[203] B.D. Thomas, *Denominational Esprit de Corps* (Philadelphia: American Baptist Publication Society, [1870s?]), 10.

For Thomas, there was only one resting place for him and those to whom he preached: "the bulwark of our strength is the word of God."[204]

From his scrapbook of newspaper clippings one gets a good idea of the range of texts on which Thomas preached, for many of the clippings are newspaper transcripts of sermons that he gave. Although Thomas does not appear to have preached through particular books as some earlier Baptists had done—men like Andrew Fuller, for example[205]—he did preach from a variety of passages throughout the Scriptures. In this method of preaching he resembled one of his heroes, his older contemporary Charles Haddon Spurgeon.[206]

Final days

Thomas resigned from the Jarvis Street pastorate in the summer of 1903. The main reasons for his doing so was simply the fact that at the age of sixty-seven Thomas found "the increasing responsibilities of the large church were becoming too heavy."[207] His retirement took him to Grimsby, Ontario, where he lived till his death on October 26, 1917. The Sunday prior to his death, he attended the worship of his old church, Jarvis Street Baptist Church, where an Englishman, T.T.

---

[204] Thomas, *Denominational Esprit de Corps*, 9. In a sermon on John 16:12–14 (Newspaper clipping in Thomas, "My Pastorate in Toronto"), Thomas asserted that "the Spirit always operates in harmony with the revealed truth and always glorifies Christ. Accept no teaching, believe in no ministry, follow no leadership which is not prepared to submit itself to these two tests."

[205] Thomas admired Fuller as one of those Baptists—he mentions him along with Carey, Robert Hall, Jr. (1764–1831), and William Knibb (1803–1845)—whose names "have not been exceeded in lustre since apostolic times" and who have "shed an undying resplendence upon our [i.e. Baptist] history" (Newspaper clipping in Thomas, "My Pastorate in Toronto").

[206] In Thomas' opinion, "no history of nineteenth century Christianity will be written in which Spurgeon and [Alexander] Maclaren will not have a foremost place" (Newspaper clipping in Thomas, "My Pastorate in Toronto"). After Spurgeon's death in 1892, Thomas gave an address at a special memorial service held for Spurgeon in Toronto. Thomas spoke on 2 Timothy 4:6 and compared Spurgeon to Paul "in his theology as well as in his consecration and enthusiasm" (Newspaper clipping in Thomas, "My Pastorate in Toronto").

[207] "Rev. Dr. Thomas Resigns" (Newspaper clipping in Thomas, "My Pastorate in Toronto").

Shields (1873-1955) was now the pastor. Thomas and Shields were similar: they were both firmly convinced that the central solution to the need of the age was the preaching of the gospel. The main reason for Thomas' being at Jarvis Street was to hear his son, Llewellyn, preach at the evening service. He died four days later. It is doubtful that he could have desired a more appropriate closing to his long life.

In a graduation address that Thomas once delivered on 1 Kings 7:22a ("Upon the tops of the pillars was lily work"), he observed:

> All Christian character is royal. The most insignificant stone in this spiritual temple [of the church] is sublime. The imperial agencies of the Holy Spirit give grandeur to the poorest lives. There is not one so low and ignorant but that brought beneath the regenerating and purifying influences of God's saving grace shall one day shine in burnished beauty. But there are some who occupy positions of special prominence and distinction; who stand forth in the broad spaces of the supernal structure as its supporting and adorning pillars.[208]

By God's grace, Benjamin Daniel Thomas had been such a pillar in Ontario.

---

[208] "Pulpit and Platform. Strength and Beauty" (Newspaper clipping in Thomas, "My Pastorate in Toronto").

Daniel Arthur McGregor

10

Daniel Arthur McGregor and "The McMaster Hymn"

♦ ♦ ♦

IF THERE IS one text that encapsulates the piety of Ontario Baptists in the Victorian era, it is the hymn "Jesus, Wondrous Saviour," sometimes known as "The McMaster Hymn." The hymn is suffused with joy and powerfully depicts what was central to the heart of its author, Daniel Arthur McGregor (1847–1890), namely, declaring the glory and beauty of Christ. McGregor, who penned the hymn not long before his death, was a product of the Scottish Baptist community of the Ottawa Valley, which, as we have seen, was a major force in the establishment of the Baptist denomination in nineteenth-century Ontario.[209]

---

[209] This chapter on D.A. McGregor is based on the *Memoir of Daniel Arthur McGregor*, [ed. A.H. Newman,] 2nd ed. (Toronto, ON: The Alumni Association of Toronto Baptist College, 1891). Newman was helped in his editorial work by McGregor's wife Augusta (who selected the tributes to her husband found in chapter VI and the various essays and sermons of his in the second half of the book), his brother Malcolm (who prepared chapters I and V), and two of his close friends, E.W. Dadson (who wrote chapter II) and D.G. MacDonald (who authored chapter III).

For short studies of his life, see also S.S. Bates, "Daniel Arthur McGregor," *The McMaster University Monthly* 5 (1895–1896): 241–247; "Concerning Principal McGregor: A Prince and a Great Man," *The Regular Baptist Call* 31, no.4 (April 1957): 7–9.

JESUS, WONDROUS SAVIOUR

McGregor in his context

Christine Blaikie, McGregor's maternal grandmother, had been converted through the ministry of the Haldane brothers, who had such a profound impact upon the Scottish Baptist community in both Scotland and Ontario, as was noted in Chapter 1. She subsequently married Malcolm McGregor, and, with her husband and two children, emigrated to Canada in 1817. They initially settled in Montreal, where Christine was drawn to the sole Baptist fellowship in that city. In fact, it was in the McGregor home that the first Baptist celebration of the Lord's Supper in Montreal was held.[210] The McGregors moved to the Ottawa Valley in 1820 and Christine eventually joined what became Dalesville Baptist Church.[211] In the mid-1830s, her husband Malcolm was converted as well as her son Alexander—the father of Daniel—during the long-remembered revival in the Ottawa Valley that we noted earlier in this book. Alexander soon thought about going into the ministry and moved back to Montreal to study at Canada Baptist College, which opened its doors in 1838. After two years of study, though, Alexander was convinced that God was not calling him to pastoral service. But for the rest of his life, he made it a matter of fervent prayer that one of his sons might be called to the pastorate.[212]

In 1842, after returning from Montreal, Alexander McGregor married Clementine McArthur (d.1876), whose family had also been profoundly shaped by the ministry of the Haldanes in Scotland. The couple eventually made their home in Osgoode township, which took its name from the first chief justice of Ontario (Upper Canada at the

---

[210] Malcolm MacGregor, "Chapter I. Ancestry and Early Life" in *Memoir of Daniel Arthur McGregor*, 10–11.

[211] For the history of this church, see George F. Calder, "Historical Sketch of Dalesville Baptist Church" (Typewritten ms., 1925) and "History of Dalesville Baptist Church" (http://dalesvillebaptistchurch.weebly.com/our-history.html and http://dalesvillebaptistchurch.weebly.com/early-history.html; accessed January 6, 2023).

[212] MacGregor, "Chapter I. Ancestry and Early Life" in *Memoir of Daniel Arthur McGregor*, 12–13.

time), William Osgoode (1754–1824).²¹³ It was here that Daniel was born in 1847, the younger of twins and the fifth child of the family. Osgoode was typical of rural Ontario at the time and Daniel had virtually no opportunities for formal schooling after the age of 12. However, he had developed a keen interest in reading, which did him in good stead during his teen years. After being led to Christ in June of 1867 by an older brother, Malcolm, and being baptized in the Castor River, he joined the Osgoode Church, which had been founded by his uncle, Daniel McPhail, in 1839. McPhail had pastored this church till 1865 when he was called to the First Baptist Church in Ottawa.²¹⁴

The Osgoode work was a remarkable church known for its piety and knowledge of the Scriptures. Of the families in the church, it was said that "every dinner table was a theological class" with the Bible as "the arbiter of the daily discussion." As one of McGregor's pastoral friends, E.W. Dadson (1845–1900), put it: "There was no escaping God and the Bible in that community."²¹⁵ It is thus no surprise that McGregor was adept at dealing with profound theological issues from his youth.²¹⁶

McGregor as student and pastor

Three years after his conversion, and with the cordial recommendation of his home church in Osgoode, McGregor left for the Canadian Literary Institute in Woodstock. MacGregor studied at Woodstock for eight years and graduated in 1878. During this time, Robert Alexander Fyfe left an indelible mark for good on McGregor's life and thought. Indeed, he always regarded Fyfe as the greatest mentor in his life.²¹⁷ During the two years after graduation, McGregor pastored Baptist churches in Whitby and Brooklin, while also studying for his B.A. at

---

[213] The famous law school in Toronto, Osgoode Hall, is also named after William Osgoode.
[214] For a sketch of McPhail's ministry, see J. Dempsey, "Daniel McPhail," *The McMaster University Monthly* 2 (1892–1893): 257–271.
[215] E.W. Dadson, "Chapter II. Student Life" in *Memoir of Daniel Arthur McGregor*, 24.
[216] Dadson, "Chapter II. Student Life" in *Memoir of Daniel Arthur McGregor*, 26.
[217] Dadson, "Chapter II. Student Life" in *Memoir of Daniel Arthur McGregor*, 33.

the University of Toronto. He obtained this degree in 1881, the same year that he moved to Stratford to pastor the Baptist work there.

In Stratford, he won the hearts of the congregation with "the magnetism of a life surcharged with the Spirit of Jesus Christ" as well as a deep reliance upon the Scriptures. This biblicism was a mark, as mentioned earlier, of the Haldanes and the Scottish congregations that they established and influenced, including McGregor's home church in Osgoode.[218] After McGregor's death there was found among his papers four sermons and eight plans of sermons on one of the central themes of Scripture, the declaration of Revelation 5:12: "Worthy is the Lamb that was slain." Here is a snippet from one of those talks. He noted that Christ's

> hatred of sin and his love of holiness caused him to enter the very charnel-house of human sin, that he might wash it from its dismal stains in his own most precious blood. The wisdom and the power displayed in his atoning work have become the wonder of the universe and of eternity. He is the power of God and the wisdom of God. In him we have all the treasures of wisdom and knowledge. In him all glories meet. He is the chiefest among ten thousand, the altogether lovely. His righteousness is not simply superior to that of all others in the kingdom. They have all discarded their own righteousness as a ground of acceptance and stand justified simply through his infinite merit. O the transcendent and the unspeakable worth of Christ.[219]

In this passage, McGregor made reference to two affirmations about Christ by Paul—found in 1 Corinthians 1:24 and Colossians 2:3—as well as to Song of Songs 5:10 ("chiefest among ten thousand" [KJV]) and 5:16 ("altogether lovely" [KJV]), which McGregor obviously understood in classic tradition as Christological passages.

By means of this Christ-centred ministry, God made him a winner of souls. Between May of 1881 and June of 1886, the years of his

---

[218] D.G. Macdonald, "Chapter III. The Pastorate" in *Memoir of Daniel Arthur McGregor*, 47–49.
[219] D.A. McGregor, "Worthy is the Lamb" in *Memoir of Daniel Arthur McGregor*, 217–218.

ministry at Stratford, 121 persons were received into the Church by baptism—another 62 joined the church "by letter and experience," a reference to the fact that their Christian lives had been initiated in another church.[220] Churches offering him a bigger salary repeatedly approached him. But he turned a deaf ear to these offers, for he did not believe his work at Stratford was finished. In June of 1886, though, Toronto Baptist College offered the professorship in homiletics to him. Recognizing God's call, he resigned the pastorate and moved to Toronto.[221] During his ministry in Stratford, in December of 1881, McGregor married Augusta Hull, who would bear five children in seven years.[222]

Homiletics was not the area of teaching that Daniel Arthur McGregor would have chosen if he had had a choice, but he undertook the work at Toronto Baptist College cheerfully. In 1888 he took on teaching apologetics and that same year he was requested to move into teaching systematic theology. Every lecture that he delivered took numerous hours of diligent preparation, for he was convinced that he should never stand in front of his students with anything but the most careful and extensive study.[223] One of his students later said of his teaching:

> He not only thought out the … doctrines upon which he lectured, but he felt their power, and falling tears often evinced his emotion while he spoke of some particular aspect of the truth. This made us all feel that we had before us not only a theological professor but also a Christian man whose life was swayed by the great principles about which he spoke. I find it hard to estimate the value of such a view of Christian doctrines. He must be a brilliant botanist who can not only give to his students a strictly accurate knowledge of flowers, but can also

---

[220] Macdonald, "Chapter III. The Pastorate" in *Memoir of Daniel Arthur McGregor*, 63.
[221] For one account of his ministry in Stratford, see Macdonald, "Chapter III. The Pastorate" in *Memoir of Daniel Arthur McGregor*, 44–65.
[222] Macdonald, "Chapter III. The Pastorate" in *Memoir of Daniel Arthur McGregor*, 58–59.
[223] A.H. Newman, "Chapter IV. Professor and Principal" in *Memoir of Daniel Arthur McGregor*, 78.

inspire in them an enthusiastic admiration for their aesthetic beauty. This was what Professor McGregor succeeded in doing. He not only made us see the truth, but he made us feel its power and perceive its beauty.[224]

During this whole time of teaching, he preached almost as much as if he had been a pastor, some of it at his home church, Immanuel Baptist Church, then located at the corner of Jarvis Street and Wellesley Street East.[225] Though warned against subjecting himself to such constant stress and strain, he neglected to heed these warnings. Compounding the stress that McGregor experienced was the death of his only son, Arthur, who succumbed to diphtheria in the early fall of 1888.[226]

In the spring of 1889, McGregor was chosen as succeed John Castle as the principal of Toronto Baptist College. He was in office only a year, though, before he succumbed to Pott's disease, a tubercular disease of the spinal column. McGregor had wrenched his back severely in 1886 when he was helping to move a piano into his Toronto residence. Physicians at the time thought this might have contributed to the onset of the disease. Symptoms of the disease showed themselves in June of 1889, when McGregor began to complain of an odd pain in his back. By August he was completely paralyzed in the lower half of his body. Eventually, he underwent an operation in New York Hospital on April 16, 1890, but complications set in and he died nine days later on April 25. His body was brought back to Toronto by his grieving widow, Augusta, and Malcolm, his eldest brother, both of whom had been at his bedside when he died. He was buried in Mount Pleasant Cemetery in Toronto.[227]

---

[224] Cited Newman, "Chapter IV. Professor and Principal" in *Memoir of Daniel Arthur McGregor*, 80–81, *passim*.

[225] For a brief mention of his membership at Immanuel, see A.C. Simmonds, *Diary of a Century: Commemorating the Centennial of Immanuel Baptist Church Toronto* (Oshawa, ON: Alger Press, 1966), 35.

[226] Macdonald, "Chapter III. The Pastorate" in *Memoir of Daniel Arthur McGregor*, 58–59; Newman, "Chapter IV. Professor and Principal" in *Memoir of Daniel Arthur McGregor*, 77.

[227] For some of the details of this paragraph, see Malcolm MacGregor, "Chapter V. Last Illness" in *Memoir of Daniel Arthur McGregor*, 94–122.

DANIEL McGREGOR AND "THE McMASTER HYMN

"The McMaster Hymn"

While confined to his bed in the principal's quarters at the east end of McMaster Hall during the season of Advent in 1889, McGregor composed a hymn that his brother Malcolm later described as "expressive of adoring love and ardent longing for the Saviour."[228] After the hymn's initial composition, it underwent at least one revision by McGregor. This revision was subsequently copied out by hand by his wife Augusta, who gave it to her husband's twin brother Robert, who, in turn, presented it to McMaster University in 1921. Eventually it came to be housed in the Canadian Baptist Archives at McMaster Divinity College.[229] In time this hymn, "Jesus, Wondrous Saviour," became known as the McMaster Hymn and was regularly sung at official McMaster University events. As noted at the very outset of this chapter, it stands as a marvelous expression of nineteenth-century Ontario Baptist piety. The full hymn runs as follows, though usually stanzas 2 and 3, are omitted when it is sung today:[230]

> Jesus, wondrous Saviour!
> Christ, of kings the King![231]
> Angels fall before Thee
> Prostrate, worshipping;[232]

---

[228] MacGregor, "Chapter V. Last Illness" in *Memoir of Daniel Arthur McGregor*, 100–102.

[229] These details regarding the hymn's composition and transmission are based on remarks made by J.J. Baker in a chapel address at McMaster University on March 21, 1929, and a note in *McMaster University/McMaster Divinity College 1989–90 and 1990–91 Calendar* (Hamilton, ON: McMaster Divinity College, 1989), ii. J.J. Baker had visited McGregor not long after the initial composition of the hymn and he recalled discussing it with the author. For his remarks, see "History of the McMaster Hymn" (Typescript ms., 2 pages, n.d.), [2]. This typescript can be found in the Canadian Baptist Archives, McMaster Divinity College, Hamilton, ON.

[230] There is very little punctuation in the original handwritten version that is housed in the Canadian Baptist Archives, McMaster Divinity College, Hamilton, ON. In the transcription below, I have followed the punctuation in the hymn's early print appearance in the "Supplement" to *The Canadian Baptist Hymnal* (Halifax: Baptist Book and Tract Society, 1899), 451–452. Certain clear biblical allusions have been noted.

[231] Revelation 17:14; 19:16.

[232] Revelation 5:14; 7:11; 5:8.

JESUS, WONDROUS SAVIOUR

Fairest they confess Thee
In the Heaven above.
We would sing Thee fairest
Here in hymns of love.

Fairer far than sunlight
Unto eyes that wait
Amid fear and darkness,
Till the morning break.
Fairer than the day-dawn,
Hills and dales among,
When its tide of glory
Wakes the tide of song.

Sweeter far than music
Quivering from keys
That unbind all feeling
With strange harmonies,
Thou art more and dearer
Than all minstrelsy.
Only in Thy presence
Can joy's fulness be.[233]

All earth's flowing pleasures
Were a wintry sea;
Heaven itself without Thee
Dark as night would be.
Lamb of God! Thy glory[234]
Is the light above.
Lamb of God! Thy glory
Is the life of love.[235]

Life is death, if severed
From Thy throbbing heart.

---

[233] Psalm 16:11.
[234] John 1:29; Revelation 5:6; 21:23.
[235] *The Canadian Baptist Hymnal* renders this line "Is Thy life of love," but the handwritten original has the line as rendered in the above transcription.

Death with life abundant[236]
At Thy touch would start.
Worlds and men and angels
All consist in Thee;[237]
Yet Thou camest to us[238]
In humility.[239]

Jesus! all perfections
Rise and end in Thee,
Brightness of God's glory[240]
Thou, eternally.
Favour'd beyond measure
They Thy face who see;
May we, gracious Saviour,
Share this ecstasy.

This supremely Christ-centred hymn begins and ends with the worship of Christ in heaven. In the first stanza, it is angelic worship that is depicted and urged as a model for human worship in this world. Stanzas 2 and 3 are, in some ways, typical of flowery Victorian poetry, but surely one can see in them the comfort that McGregor drew from the person of Christ during the times of "fear and darkness" during the season of Advent in 1889. His hope was an eschatological one: the enjoyment of Christ in the world to come. These two stanzas build to the climax at the close of the third stanza: "Only in Thy presence/Can joy's fulness be."

---

[236] *The Canadian Baptist Hymnal* renders this line "Death to life abundant," but the handwritten original employs the preposition "with" instead of "to."

[237] Colossians 1:17. The McMaster motto, τὰ πάντα ἐν αὐτῷ συνέστηκεν, was drawn from this verse.

[238] The original manuscript might read "comest" rather than "camest." As George Peel Gilmour (1900–1963), one-time President of McMaster University, noted: "it is a tossup whether in stanza 5, line 7 the manuscript reads "comest" or "camest." Logic demands the latter" (Letter to D'Alton McLaughlin, November 17, 1960 [Canadian Baptist Archives, McMaster Divinity College, Hamilton, ON]).

[239] Matthew 11:29; Philippians 2:7–8.

[240] Hebrews 1:3.

The fourth stanza takes it rise from this conclusion, which might be a good reason for not omitting stanzas 2 or 3 when singing this hymn. Compared to the joy of being in Christ's actual presence, all of the pleasures of this world (and McGregor's words in stanzas 2 and 3 clearly indicated that he enjoyed earthly pleasures) are like the harshness of a winter's sea. In fact, the hymnist goes on to say, heaven itself would be robbed of its light and glory if Christ were not in it.

The word "life" at the close of the fourth stanza is what is picked up by stanza 5, a profound mini-reflection on death and life. True death precedes physical death for those not joined to Christ and physical death is not really death if the one dying is a Christian. Death and life are thus ultimately not merely physical states, but spiritual ones. And what McGregor found amazing is that the One who gives the true life that triumphs over death, the One who sustains the entire universe (a clear reference to Colossians 1:17, which became the motto of McMaster University), came into this world "in humility" and human frailty. He was obviously thinking here of Philippians 2, and its great hymn to Christ.

The first four lines of Stanza 5 are also reminiscent of some lines from an earlier hymnwriter, the Evangelical Anglican minister, Augustus Montague Toplady (1740–1778), whose name and hymns would have been quite familiar to McGregor. The third stanza of Toplady's hymn "Happiness, thou lovely name," (1774) runs thus:

> Lord it is not life to live,
> If Thy presence Thou deny;
> Lord, if Thou Thy presence give,
> 'Tis no longer death to die.

McGregor would have known these lines as part of the hymn "Object of my first desire," a shortened version of Toplady's hymn that was printed in *The Canadian Baptist Hymn Book* (1873) and that would have been used for worship at the Canadian Literary Institute.[241] R.A. Fyfe

---

[241] For this rendition of "Object of my first desire," see *The Canadian Baptist Hymn Book* (Toronto, ON: Copp, Clark, & Co., 1873), 188, Hymn #323. For Fyfe's involvement in editing this hymnal, see *Canadian Baptist Hymn Book*, "Prefatory Note."

was one of the editors of this hymnal. In fact, for this expression of his thought, McGregor was probably also reliant upon the Seventh-day Baptist hymn writer Joseph Stennett I (1663–1713), who, with Isaac Watts (1674–1748), stands at the fountainhead of English Evangelical hymnody. In a dedicatory poem to his *Hymns In Commemoration Of the Sufferings of Our Blessed Saviour Jesus Christ, Compos'd For the Celebration of his Holy Supper* (1709), which begins thus, "O Thou whom Angels with their Hymns address," Stennett declared:

> Life will be Death, if I am exil'd from Thee;
> Death will be Life, if I Thy face may see.[242]

The possibility that McGregor was drawing upon this early Baptist pioneer of hymnody is strengthened when one sees the similarity between the final phrase of this quote from Stennett's poem and line 6 of McGregor's final stanza.

The final stanza continues to laud Christ—now in words drawn from Hebrews 1—and ends where the hymn began: in the glory of the heavenly worship of Jesus. In the face of all of his suffering, McGregor had this prayerful hope: to see the face of his "gracious Saviour." This is true "ecstasy," of which the pleasures in this world are pale reflections.

Reflecting Victorian Baptist piety in Ontario

Though written by a man dealing with profound suffering, this hymn is suffused with joy in Christ and the conviction that only in the glory of his presence can he, as a human being, know the height of human pleasure. In the face of such pain, these verses became McGregor's personal confession of faith in a risen, glorified Saviour.[243] Given McGregor's probable reading of Stennett and possibly also Toplady, it is evident that McGregor has drawn creatively upon the rich hymnic

---

[242] Joseph Stennett, "The Dedication" in his *Hymns In Commemoration Of the Sufferings of Our Blessed Saviour Jesus Christ, Compos'd For the Celebration of his Holy Supper*, 3rd ed. (London: John Baker, 1709), xxxvi.
[243] Gordon Carder, "We Would Sing Thee Fairest Here in Hymns," *The Canadian Baptist* 133, no.5 (May 1987): "In his hours of terrible trial these lines [of "Jesus, Wondrous Saviour"] became McGregor's affirmation of faith."

JESUS, WONDROUS SAVIOUR

tradition of Evangelicalism to create a Christ-centred hymn that well sums up the way in which Ontario Baptists sought to intertwine piety and theology at the close of the Victorian era.

Toronto Baptist Seminary

11

T.T. Shields and the Importance of Learning

♦ ♦ ♦

IN THE SECOND issue of *The Gospel Witness*—the church magazine of Jarvis Street Baptist Church that was launched in the early 1920s—the paper's editor, T.T. Shields, asked his readers to pray for what were then the two leading Baptist schools in Canada: Acadia University in Wolfville, Nova Scotia, and McMaster University, still located at that time on Bloor Street, Toronto, only a short distance away from the headquarters of *The Gospel Witness* in Jarvis Street Baptist Church, where Shields was the pastor. The need for prayer was especially acute since Acadia was seeking a new president and McMaster had to find a new Chancellor to replace Abraham Lincoln McCrimmon (1865–1935), who had occupied that position since 1911 and had stepped down earlier in 1922. Shields noted that the "future of Canadian Baptists is to a large degree involved in the history" of these two schools, a clear indication of the importance he placed on education. "May these schools," Shields asked his readers to pray, "have the light and learning that come from our Lord Who is the Light of the world and its only Redeemer."[244]

---

[244] "Acadia as well as McMaster," *The Gospel Witness* 1, no.2 (March 27, 1922): 7. For the life and ministry of T.T. Shields, see especially Arnold Dallimore, "T.T. Shields," *Reformation Today* 86 (July–August 1985). 7–10, Leslie K. Tarr, *Shields of Canada: T.T. Shields (1873–1955)* (Grand Rapids, MI: Baker Book House, 1967); idem, "Another Perspective on T.T. Shields and Fundamentalism" in Jarold K. Zeman, ed., *Baptists in Canada: Search for Identity Amidst Diversity* (Burlington, ON: G. R. Welch Co., Ltd., 1980), 209–224; G.A. Rawlyk, "A.L. McCrimmon, H.P.

Within four years of his penning this prayer, though, Shields felt himself compelled to open a new seminary under the auspices of the Jarvis Street congregation. In a note that appeared in *The Gospel Witness* under the heading "The Toronto Baptist Seminary," he stated that he regretted "the necessity for this venture." However, he declared, concern about "the poison [being] disseminated through the teaching of McMaster" in its theological department as well as the spirit, or ambience, of McMaster, made such a move necessary.[245] Lying between Shields' prayer in the spring of 1922 and his decision in late 1926 to open another school were a couple of key events at McMaster which convinced Shields that the Baptist school on Bloor Street was definitely heading in a liberal direction.

The Fundamentalist-Modernist Controversy

First, there was McMaster's granting of a doctorate *honoris causa* to W.H.P. Faunce (1859–1930), the President of Brown University, the oldest Baptist institution of higher learning in North America, but a man who was also well-known as a liberal in his theological commitments.[246] The conferral of the degree took place at the installation of Howard Primrose Whidden (1870–1952) on November 12, 1923, who succeeded McCrimmon as McMaster's sixth chancellor. When Shields protested at the granting of this degree to such a known liberal, both Whidden and Jones Hughes Farmer (1859–1928), the Dean of Theology, pleaded ignorance of Faunce's theological pedigree. In a letter written on November 24, Whidden expressly told

---

Whidden, T.T. Shields, Christian Education, and McMaster University" in his ed., *Canadian Baptists and Christian Higher Education* (Kingston, ON; Montreal, QC: McGill-Queen's University Press, 1988), 31–62; Doug A. Adams, "The War of the Worlds: The Militant Fundamentalism of Dr. Thomas Todhunter Shields and the Paradox of Modernity" (PhD thesis, The University of Western Ontario, 2015).

[245] T.T. Shields, "The Toronto Baptist Seminary," *The Gospel Witness* 5, no.32 (December 16, 1926): 22–23.

[246] For an excellent overview of Faunce's commitment to liberal theology, see Jeffrey Paul Straub, *The Making of a Battle Royal: The Rise of Liberalism in Northern Baptist Life, 1870–1920* (Eugene, OR: Pickwick Publications, 2018), especially 291–297.

Shields that "probably the members of the [McMaster] Senate had never read a theological statement by Dr. Faunce. I, myself, had not seen any of his pamphlets." After all, Whidden added, it was the institution of which Faunce was the president that was being honoured, not the man.[247] But Shields rightly regarded these explanations as utterly inadequate: should not the university have enquired into the theological convictions of a man whom they were honouring in such a way?[248]

Second, and more significantly, there had been McMaster's appointment in 1925 of Laurance Henry Marshall (1882–1953) as Professor of Practical Theology.[249] Marshall was an Englishman with an extremely winsome personality and powerful pulpit presence. The church that he pastored in England before coming to Canada—Queen's Road Baptist Church, Coventry, the largest Baptist work at the time in the Midlands—long remembered him as a pulpit orator, whose style was reminiscent of some of the great Victorian preachers. Henry Bonser, who wrote a memoir of Marshall after his death, described him as "pre-eminently a preacher with a message."[250] In fact, when Frederick Griffin, an experienced reporter with *The Toronto Star* in the 1920s, heard Marshall speak at the tumultuous national convention of the Canadian Baptists in 1926, he felt he had only ever heard another talk equal to Marshall's "flaming, magnificent speech" and that was a speech given by the Canadian Prime Minister, Wilfrid Laurier.

---

[247] H.P. Whidden, Letter to T. T. Shields, November 24, 1923 (T.T. Shields Letters, Jarvis Street Baptist Church Archives, Jarvis Street Baptist Church, Toronto, ON).

[248] Charles M. Johnston, *McMaster University Volume 1/The Toronto Years* (Toronto, ON; Buffalo, NY: University of Toronto Press for McMaster University, 1976), 174–176.

[249] For an overview of Marshall's life and career, see Henry Bonser, "A Memoir of the Author: Laurance Henry Marshall 1882–1953" in L.H. Marshall, *Rivals of the Christian Faith* (London: Carey Kingsgate Press, 1954), 1–15. For a clear statement of his theological convictions, see his "Religious Controversy in Canada," *The Fraternal and Remembrancer*, n.s. 1 (January 1931): 6–11. On his theological views, see also Barry D. Smith, "Was Laurence H. Marshall really a Modernist?" (Typescript ms., n.d., in the possession of the author).

[250] Bonser, "Laurance Henry Marshall," 9.

JESUS, WONDROUS SAVIOUR

Yet, there is no doubt that Marshall had definitely imbibed significant doses of liberal thinking. In an article written a few years after the controversy, Marshall declared his support for the theory of evolution, his rejection of the infallibility of God's Word, and his intense dislike of viewing the death of the Lord Jesus as a vicarious punishment for the sins of his people. Marshall seems to have regarded the message of Scripture as inspired, but not the text itself.[251] As he once remarked, "Religion is in men not in manuscripts."[252] And as he also told W.S. Whitcombe (1905–1990), an inerrantist who later taught at Toronto Baptist Seminary for many years, "Mr. Whitcombe, your attitude to the Bible and mine are poles apart."[253] And with regard to the doctrine of the atonement, Marshall saw the crucifixion of Christ as the supreme example of divine love, but not a propitiation for the sins of sinners. There is also evidence that Marshall was not entirely comfortable with affirming the bodily resurrection of Christ. At the time of his appointment, however, McMaster's administration, especially Farmer and Whidden, were adamant that Marshall was orthodox.

Farmer's defence of Marshall was odd, for Farmer was a man who rightly declared in Lindsay Baptist Church (now Cambridge Street Baptist Church), in November, 1927, that he had steadily opposed "any type of Modernism that would take the crown from the brow of Jesus Christ."[254] And as W.S. Whitcombe later noted, Farmer was

> a man who loved the Word and whose classes in the New Testament were times of spiritual refreshing. There was no room for questioning his sincere devotion to the great truths of the gospel. Nevertheless, he warmly defended the succession of liberal teachers in his department and argued that since the university accepted financial support from certain wealthy men who espoused the new theology [i.e. liberalism], it was only just

---

[251] See Marshall, "Religious Controversy in Canada," 9.
[252] Cited J.H. Watt, *The Fellowship Story: Our First 25 Years* ([Willowdale, ON]: The Fellowship of Evangelical Baptist Churches in Canada, 1978), 24–25.
[253] Cited Watt, *The Fellowship Story*, 25.
[254] "Meeting of Drs. Farmer and MacNeill and Mr. Duncan at Lindsay—November 2nd, 1927" (Typescript ms., Jarvis Street Baptist Church Archives, Toronto, Ontario).

and fair that a place should be found for their theology in the classrooms.[255]

It was Shields' commitment to the centrality of biblical authority that drew him into public criticism of Marshall and of the McMaster administration for defending the liberal professor. For two years, between the Ontario and Quebec Baptist conventions of 1925 and 1927, what can be described as "all-out war"—by means of the spoken word, the printed page, and various rallies throughout Ontario—raged relentlessly between Shields and his supporters and those siding with the McMaster administration and Marshall. Shields attacked his opponents in the pages of *The Gospel Witness*, as well as from the pulpit of Jarvis Street. Rallies in support of both sides were held and numerous pamphlets published.

Was it simply Shields' abrasive character or even his overweening ambition that lay at the bottom of his dogged involvement in this struggle? For instance, one contemporary, F.F. MacNab, called Shields the "Pope of Jarvis Street."[256] Even friends of Shields admitted that there were times when Shields was abrasive and domineering.[257] For instance, in the late 1940s, Shields clashed with W. Gordon Brown (1904–1979), who had stood side-by-side with Shields during the controversy of the 1920s. This clash eventuated in a substantial division between the two men and the formation of a new seminary, Central Baptist Seminary in Toronto. During this controversy between Shields and Brown, two of Shields' former students, Arnold A. Dallimore (1911–1998) and Hal MacBain (1916–2016), corresponded about it. Dallimore, who was in New York at the time, wrote to his close friend the following about Shields:

---

[255] "A Word from W.S. Whitcombe," *The Evangelical Baptist* 35, no.8 (June 1988): 11.
[256] "An Unfortunate Necessity," *The McMaster Graduate* 5, no.3 (December 1925), 16.
[257] J.R. Boyd, "An Alumnus Remembers" in *By His Grace To His Glory: 60 Years of Ministry* (Toronto, ON: Toronto Baptist Seminary and Bible College, 1987), 91. See also Tarr, "Another Perspective on T.T. Shields," 222.

> As far as preach[ing] goes, T.T.S. is incomparably above anything I have heard here [in New York]. ...It makes it all the more evident that T.T. might have been everywhere recognized as the leader of evangelicals,—if he had only lost his big shot attitude; if he had more of what many lesser men have— Christian kindness, humility, love, grace![258]

But the controversy of the 1920s was not ultimately about personalities, but faithfulness to God's truth. As Leslie K. Tarr once asked: "Even if Shields was abrasive and provocative, does that in itself invalidate his accusations?"[259] In the final analysis, it must be recognized that it was Shields' fidelity to biblical truth that did so much to prevent the dilution of the Baptist testimony in Ontario and Quebec.[260] The controversy over Marshall's theological convictions came to a head in 1927. The Baptist Convention of Ontario and Quebec expelled Jarvis Street Baptist Church and twelve other congregations who had sided with Shields.

The importance of learning

Now, Shields' change of mind with regard to McMaster was interpreted by his major antagonists as sure evidence of a love of ignorance and obscurantism. Marshall asked the Ontario and Quebec Baptist church delegates at their annual convention in 1927, in which Marshall was exonerated:

> Are we as Baptists to stand for ignorance and obscurantism and intolerance, or are we to get into line with all the truly great men whose names are written upon our Baptist roll of fame, (and the greatest of them all in my humble opinion is Wm. Carey the great pioneer of modern missionary enterprise) and stand for sound scholarship, for the love of truth, for tolerance, for

---

[258] Arnold A. Dallimore, Letter to Hall MacBain, August 11, 1949 ("Dally's Dilemmas," MacBain Personal Archives in the possession of Alan and Grave Silvester of Tillsonburg, ON).
[259] Tarr, "Another Perspective on T.T. Shields," 214.
[260] Tarr, "Another Perspective on T.T. Shields," 223.

reasonable liberty, with the McMaster motto as our watchword: "In Christ all things consist."[261]

Marshall's claim to be standing in the line of "all the truly great men" of the Baptist past—in particular, William Carey, one of the leading pioneers of the modern missionary movement—reveals his conviction that his brand of non-confessional Baptist theology was the norm in Baptist history.[262] But this was not actually the case. Four years later, after Marshall had returned to England, he reiterated his charge against Shields in an English Baptist quarterly. Shields' Fundamentalism was one of "darkness and obscurantism" that was born out of a "fear of criticism, [and] fear of scholarship." "If only he had been well educated," Marshall lamented, "he might have been one of the most powerful ministers of the gospel of Christ on the American continent."[263]

However, Marshall's analysis of his theological opponent was altogether wrong. The issue at stake between Marshall the Modernist Baptist and Shields the Fundamentalist Baptist cannot be resolved merely in terms of a difference with regard to the value placed upon education in general or theological education in particular. To be sure, there had been among the Ontario Baptists, as among their co-religionists in the United Kingdom and the United States, those who had a basic distrust of theological education.[264] But Shields and his key supporters, men like C.J. Loney (1880–1966)—long-time pastor of Stanley Avenue Baptist Church, Hamilton, Ontario—and W. Gordon

---

[261] *The Faith of Prof. L. H. Marshall* (Toronto: [McMaster University], 1927), 23–24.
[262] It is noteworthy that in an earlier phase of the Fundamentalist-Modernist controversy among Ontario Baptists, when McMaster's Old Testament Professor Isaac George Matthews (1871–1959) was accused of liberalism in 1909–1910 by Elmore Harris (1854–1912), the founding pastor of Walmer Road Baptist Church, Toronto, Matthews also claimed to be "in harmony with the great fundamental principles of the great Baptist Brotherhood of history" in *Address by Professor Matthews* (Toronto: Standard Publishing Co., [1910]), 12.
[263] Marshall, "Religious Controversy in Canada," 10–11.
[264] See above, Chapter 3.

Brown—the founding Dean of Central Baptist Seminary, Toronto, Ontario—cannot be numbered among them.[265]

What Shields opposed was not scholarship per se, but "the arrogant assumptions of an unbelieving scholarship."[266] For Shields, a distinct Christian perspective needed to permeate every sphere of knowledge, both secular and sacred. In an article that he wrote about Christian education in 1922, he asserted in no uncertain terms:

> The Baptist view is that a Christian is a Christian everywhere, and in all things; that if a man confesses that Jesus Christ is his Lord, his subjection to Christ will color even his thinking, and that then, no matter what subject he may teach, whether it be history, or science, or language, or literature, or psychology, or sociology, or political economy, or theology he will view everything from a Christian standpoint, and there will be a savor of Christ in all his teaching: and his devotion to Christ will compound the principles of the gospel into a precious nard which will become diffused by His presence until the house is filled with the odor of the ointment: and the very atmosphere becomes charged with spiritual vitality.[267]

This "educational ideal" stands in marked contrast to the philosophy of education of Chancellor Whidden, one of Shields' main opponents during the McMaster controversy. A key source for understanding Whidden's perspective on education is his inaugural address of

---

[265] See Colin Robert Godwin, "Fundamentalist/Modernist Schism in the Baptist Convention of Ontario and Quebec, 1927–1933: An Examination of Ministerial Education" (M.Div. Seminar Project in Baptist History, McMaster University, 1996). A copy of this essay is in the Canadian Baptist Archives, McMaster Divinity College, Hamilton, Ontario. On Loney, see Michael A. G. Haykin, ed., *"Lord God, Our Thanks to Thee We Raise." The Minute Books of Stanley Avenue Baptist Church, Hamilton, 1889–1929. A Centennial Volume* (Hamilton, ON: Stanley Avenue Baptist Church, 1989), *passim*. For Brown, see Kenneth E. Hall, comp., "Dr. W. Gordon Brown: A Biography" (Typescript ms., 1965; copies in Heritage Theological Seminary, Cambridge, ON, and in the possession of the author).

[266] T.T. Shields, "The Baptist Bible Union University of Des Moines," *The Gospel Witness* 6, no.6 (June 16, 1927): 15. This article in *The Gospel Witness* was reproduced over the years in successive issues of the prospectus of Toronto Baptist Seminary.

[267] T.T. Shields, "Can we have "Baptist" Education?," *The Gospel Witness* 1, no.21 (October 5, 1922): 2.

November 1923.[268] In a printed version of the address the name of Christ is mentioned but once.[269] Nor is allusion made to the McMaster motto, τὰ πάντα ἐν Χριστῷ συνέστηκεν ("In him [Christ] all things consist," Colossians 1:17). What is highlighted by italics in the published version of this brief address was Whidden's understanding of the purpose of the education at McMaster: "Liberal education should seek to relate the individual to his universe."[270] Little wonder that Shields felt things were awry at the Baptist school up the road from Jarvis Street.

Founding Toronto Baptist Seminary

Shields' founding of what became Toronto Baptist Seminary in 1927 is further evidence of his convictions regarding the importance of education, in this case in the realm of theology. "We are in fullest agreement," he declared in 1922, "with the demand for an educated ministry." The following year, Shields was adamant that "an educated Ministry is necessary to the Church's welfare."[271]

Given his Christocentric vision of education in general, it is not surprising that when Shields came to draw up a prospectus for Toronto Baptist Seminary he found his educational ideal for the new school well captured in Paul's words in Philippians 3:8: "I count all things but loss for the excellency of the knowledge of Christ Jesus my Lord." As Shields went on to elaborate:

> The Apostle Paul was a gifted man by nature. He was a man of keen, vigorous, massive intellect. Moreover, his natural powers had developed to the full, through the highest culture which the schools of his day could provide. Even an enemy recognized that he was a man of "much learning". But when this great scholar was converted, he joyfully laid all his great abilities at the feet of Christ.

---

[268] In the following analysis of Whidden, I am indebted to Rawlyk, "A. L. McCrimmon, H. P. Whidden, T. T. Shields," 50–54.
[269] For this printed version, see H. P. Whidden, "What is a Liberal Education?," *The Canadian Journal of Religious Thought* 1 (1924): 36–39.
[270] Whidden, "What is a Liberal Education?," 39.
[271] T.T. Shields, "How to Improve McMaster," *The Gospel Witness* 1, no.22 (October 12, 1922): 4; *idem, A Call to Arms!* (N.p.: The Executive Committee of The Baptist Bible Union of North America, [1923]), 16.

> He explicitly declared that even his every thought was brought into captivity to the obedience of Christ; and in the verse we have quoted he discloses the great motive and aim of his life. He esteemed the knowledge of Christ to be the most excellent of all sciences, and tells us that it had become the rule of his life to subordinate every consideration to this one supreme end, to count everything "but loss for the excellency of the knowledge of Christ Jesus my Lord". We believe, therefore, that this represents the Christian ideal of education: Christ must be put first, the end of all education must be to know Him better. If we study languages, mathematics, literature, history, or any of the sciences, it must be with a view to obtaining a better knowledge of Christ.[272]

Moreover, in order that this Christocentric vision of theological education might be realized, Shields was convinced that the school needed to be tightly connected to a local church, in this case, Jarvis Street Baptist Church. To shut men up to the realm of theory with no practical outlet was to cause their spiritual muscles to atrophy through disuse. Growing knowledge of Christ was to be attained in the "healthy spiritual atmosphere" of the one key New Testament institution that God established, namely, the local church. Shields did note that other Toronto churches, "accepting the same distinctive principles and standards" as Jarvis Street would be involved in the theological training of the students. They stand, he said, "in relation to the Seminary very much as a number of hospitals stand in relation to a medical school."[273]

In laying out the programme of study at the new seminary Shields noted that her "great aim" was to produce preachers who will "preach the Bible as the Word of God with the same confidence as characterized the New Testament speakers and writers in their use of the Old Testament Scriptures."[274] The seminary course of study thus included not only the normal theological subjects, but also English language and literature that the "preacher of the gospel" might obtain "a thorough mastery of the languages in which he is to preach." As

---

[272] Shields, "Toronto Baptist Seminary," 34.
[273] Shields, "Toronto Baptist Seminary," 36.
[274] Shields, "Toronto Baptist Seminary," 47, 40.

Shields added: "There is a grace of the lips, as well as a preparation of the heart, required of every Christian who would be used of the Holy Spirit."[275] Here Shields was following his hero, C.H. Spurgeon, who also emphasized the learning of English at his Pastors' College.

It is noteworthy that Shields did not make the production of apologists the "great aim" of the seminary curriculum. In fact, some years earlier, Shields had actually stated:

> We believe ... that the soul cannot be nourished by contention. It is necessary to do battle for the truth, and we are resolved, therefore, to put our utmost energy into this holy war. But an army on the march needs food as urgently as munitions.[276]

Nearly ten years after these words were written, a meeting took place in 1932 between Shields and the Welsh preacher Martyn Lloyd-Jones (1899-1981).[277] In the course of their meeting Lloyd-Jones raised the question of Shields' extensive use of polemic in preaching. According to Lloyd-Jones' account, Shields defended his style of preaching with a variety of arguments, all of which Lloyd-Jones was able to refute. As their conversation drew to a close, Lloyd-Jones reportedly urged Shields:

> Dr Shields, you used to be known as the Canadian Spurgeon, and you were. You are an outstanding man, in intellect, in preaching gift, in every other respect, but over the McMaster University business in the early twenties you suddenly changed and became negatory and denunciatory. I feel it has ruined your ministry. Why don't you come back! Drop all this, preach the gospel to people positively and win them![278]

Legitimate questions have been raised about the way in which this conversation has been recorded, including the implication in the passage cited above that Shields had lost all perspective on what was to be central in preaching, namely, the Scriptures. A quick perusal of

---

[275] Shields, "Toronto Baptist Seminary," 40.
[276] Shields, *A Call to Arms!*, 9.
[277] D. Martyn Lloyd-Jones, *Preaching and Preachers* (Grand Rapids, MI: Zondervan, 1972), 258–261; Iain H. Murray, *David Martyn Lloyd-Jones: The First Forty Years 1899–1939* (Edinburgh; Carlisle, PA: Banner of Truth, 1982), 271–274.
[278] Murray, *David Martyn Lloyd-Jones*, 273.

his sermons during this period of time—many of which can be found in *The Gospel Witness*—will certainly reveal much polemic, possibly too much, but there was also a steady diet of solid Bible, and this the Lord honoured. And if one considers the graduates of the seminary in these early years, they were, above all, Bible preachers.

Finally, the seminary was to be confessional in orientation. As the seminary statement of faith Shields used a confession of faith that was a modification of the New Hampshire Confession (1833/1853), which had a distinctly Calvinistic and Baptistic emphasis. All of those teaching at the school had to wholeheartedly subscribe to this confession.

Shields' vision for theological education was Christ-centred, grounded in a doctrinal orthodoxy derived from the Scriptures, and focused on producing men of God who could point sinners to the Christ on whose propitiatory death and perfect righteousness they could rest their souls. It was a vision that Ontario Baptists from William Fraser to Daniel Arthur McGregor would have ardently and joyfully endorsed.

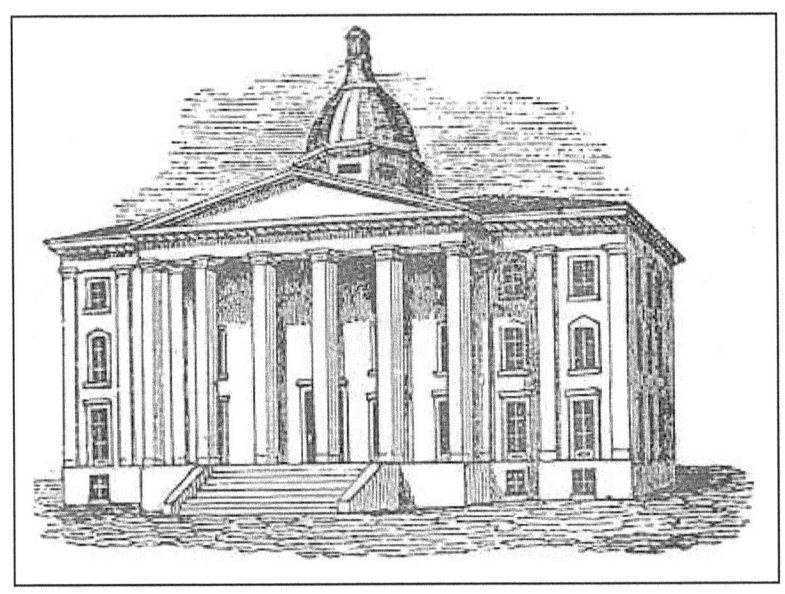

Canada Baptist College

Appendix 1

Benjamin Davies, "The Importance of Education for Those who Undertake the Work of the Ministry"[279]

The Ministers and Delegates, assembled in Association at St. Andrews, on the 22nd day of January 1840, to the Churches which they represent, send greeting.

Dearly beloved brethren: As it has pleased Him, who has been made head over all things to the church, to bring us together at this yearly season, when it is our privilege to hold fraternal intercourse and our duty to devise measures for promoting the peace and usefulness of our religious community, we think it meet to call your attention to a matter of great moment, as it regards the success and stability of the sacred cause.

We pray you then to give your candid and Christian consideration to the subject of this year's epistle, viz., *The Importance of Education for Those who Undertake the Work of the Ministry*.

This may seem to many not a suitable subject for a Circular Letter; yet our present circumstances justify the selection. There are doubtless many among us, who have not hitherto considered this matter and felt its importance, and it is to be feared there are some, who look upon it with jealousy, if not with hostility. But at the same time there is among us a theological institution,[280] which cannot be adequately supported

---

[279] From *The Canada Baptist Magazine* 3, no.9 (March 1840): 193–200. Benjamin Davies' circular letter was the fifth annual circular letter sent out by the Ottawa Baptist Association. The moderator of the session that approved this letter was William Fraser. I have utilized the transcription of this letter by Jordan A. Senécal, the librarian of Heritage Theological Seminary in Cambridge, ON. See https://bapthist.wordpress.com/2020/04/26/benjamin-davies-ministerial-education/#_ftn2. I have modernized the punctuation and capitalization of the letter as well as adding some of the biblical references.

[280] I.e., Canada Baptist College.

without the countenance and liberality of the fraternity in general. How then can such a support be secured unless the indifference of some and the opposition of others be removed? When therefore we endeavour to effect the removal of these evils, it cannot be deemed foreign from the design of the annual epistle. As the object of every Christian confederacy, whether of individuals in churches or of churches in associations, should be the advancement of religion, it cannot be inconsistent with the purpose of the present yearly meeting of the churches to invite the attention of the members to the importance of securing a well-informed ministry.

As the present subject is novel to many, it is necessary, in order to prevent misapprehension and to remove some common mistakes and prejudices, to state distinctly, before we attempt to show the importance of education for ministers, what we mean by education, and also what we do not contend for while urging its importance.

By education then we mean the literary training in various degrees, from the lowest, which consists chiefly in the ability to speak and write the English language with propriety, to the highest that can be reached by the human mind. No minister in the present day deserves to be called educated unless he is at least master of his own language. The epithet cannot be properly applied to one of less attainment; and even this application of it is not customary, for it generally implies extensive and varied attainments. The education, which we think it desirable for ministers in general to possess, consists in a knowledge of the original languages of the Scriptures (in addition to a good command of their own), in a familiarity with the principal branches of biblical literature, and in mental discipline as the result of studying mathematics, logic, and other scientific subjects.

It is then for education in the sense now explained that we wish to plead; but in doing so, we desire to disclaim certain extravagant and erroneous opinions that are held by some advocates of an enlightened ministry.

APPENDIX 1

1. We do not mean to contend that none can be worthy and useful ministers without education.

This we cannot assert, because numerous examples both in ancient and in modern times show the contrary. The first preachers of our Faith are well known examples of this kind; for many of them were destitute of literary culture, though they were made ambassadors for Christ, who honoured them with his confidence and counted them faithful, putting them into the ministry. The Apostles cannot however be compared with common illiterate men, because they had the gift of inspiration, which served as a miraculous substitute for learning to remove their ignorance or to counteract its effects. A special assurance was given to them that the Spirit should lead them to all the truth, which was also fulfilled in a supernatural manner.[281] Under the influence of this divine guidance and impulse, several of them composed well written epistles or treatises, and that too in Greek, which was not their mother tongue. Both Peter and John, the very men whom the Jewish rulers pronounced unlearned and ignorant,[282] became afterwards Greek authors; and of the other Galileans, Matthew, James, and Jude, and perhaps some besides, wrote as they were moved by the Holy Ghost. Hence it may be seen that the want of literary attainments in many of the Apostles cannot be justly urged as an argument against an educated ministry. It is often inferred by the opponents of education, that as the Apostles could succeed without it, so may the religious teachers of the present day. But it must be evident to any considerate person that such an inference is unjust, because the gift of inspiration is no longer dispensed. If indeed our pastors and missionaries enjoyed the same special and miraculous assistance as the first teachers, then it is very possible that they too might excel without possessing the advantages of human tuition. But it may be questioned whether education would not have been of some value even to the Apostles, highly favored as they were. Is it not at least a remarkable fact that much more than half the New Testament was composed by learned men, viz. Paul and Luke, the former of whom was trained at

---

[281] See John 16:13.
[282] Acts 4:13.

the feet of Gamaliel, and the latter educated for the medical profession? Is not this fact a plain indication that even in the case of inspired men, literary training contributed not a little to increase usefulness? Why else should the Apostle of the Gentiles and the beloved physician have excelled as sacred penmen? Why should they have done more than all the others put together for the instruction and stability of the church in every subsequent age, except because their erudition proved a useful handmaid to their spiritual gifts?

But not to dwell longer on the case of those extraordinary men, it is cheerfully and thankfully admitted, that many, who could lay claim to neither inspiration nor education, have proved great blessings in the ministry. There is a goodly number of such men, well known and deservedly esteemed, among us. Even some of the very Fathers of our community belong to this class. Far be it then from us to detract from the worth and services of those honoured men, whose praise is in all the churches. But yet it will always be found on examination, that the usefulness of such individuals is owing either to their possessing genius or to their laboring among people as uncultivated as themselves. A few may become eminent in consequence of possessing genius, which can amply compensate for the want of education, as was the case with John Bunyan, whose natural powers of mind made the untutored tinker, a mighty preacher and an immortal author. But the generality succeed in the ministry, chiefly because the persons, whose good they mostly seek, are too uncultivated to detect and dislike their improprieties of speech and their crudities of thought. They never can collect and edify an intelligent congregation, who require in the teachers at least as much cultivation as they themselves possess. Illiterate preachers may be exceedingly useful among illiterate people; perhaps even more useful than some others could be, who are eminent for learning. But yet the acknowledged worth of many unlettered ministers cannot be a reason for withholding literary culture from devoted men who wish to serve God in the Gospel of his Son; because these very ministers are often heard lamenting their deficiencies, and coveting learning as a help for them in their work, and many of them have been known to toil hard for years in order to inform and improve their minds, till at length by self-teaching they became capable of interesting the most cultivated hearers and of distinguishing themselves as theological writers. Of this we have a bright example in Andrew Fuller, of blessed memory, who began to preach when very unlearned, but who was so sensible of his disadvantages that he used great diligence to acquire that knowledge, without which he could never be, what he at length became—one of the most valuable men of his time and decidedly the most useful minister in our religious community.

2. *We do not mean, on the other hand, to contend that education alone, apart from moral adaptation, can qualify for the ministry.*

There are indeed multitudes who speak of training for the sacred office, in the same terms as they do of any other professional education, vainly supposing that as learning may make a lawyer, so it may also a minister. It is a notorious fact that in all secular or state churches, young men are raised to undertake "the care of souls" without any regard to their religious feelings. We however utterly reprobate such a notion and such a custom. Much as we desire a *learned* ministry, we desire a *pious* ministry more. The first and most essential qualification, which we look for and demand, is godliness, while we seek learning only as a secondary, though not unimportant preparation. It is our solemn conviction that no literary attainments, no powers of rhetoric, can give fitness for the work, if the heart be not engaged in it. This preparation of the heart in man must come from the Lord, before any other preparation, whether of erudition or of eloquence, can qualify him for the ministry. Let not one then charge us with the sacrilegious intent of making learning a substitute for piety in the teachers of our churches.

3. *We do not mean to contend for education in a theological institution to the exclusion or disparagement of that which may be obtained in any other way.*

We desire intelligence and cultivation in general without laying much stress on the place or manner in which they may be acquired; though we feel a preference for the training given in what may be called "the schools of the prophets," since it is likely to be more suitable and valuable, as having a more special and direct bearing on ministerial duties. But if the learning itself be sound and to the purpose, we care not much whether it has been gained at home, or in the collegiate seats of liberal education, or in the halls of divinity. A multitude of honored names might be mentioned of self-taught men, who forced their way to literary eminence and commanded the admiration, if not provoked the envy, of the more favored cultivators of letters, who could boast of the advantages and honors of renowned universities. Who does not know the history of our illustrious [William] Carey, how he became a prodigy of learning, without having ever frequented the groves of *Academus*? How happy a circumstance would it be for the cause of truth, if unlettered ministers generally were to follow the bright example of Carey, Fuller, [Abraham] Booth and others, by struggling through their difficulties and placing themselves on a level with the well instructed and enlightened! But alas! this is too much to expect. Some indeed are known to be making the most praiseworthy efforts for this purpose; yet while we heartily wish them success, we feel persuaded that under existing circumstances, an educated ministry cannot be secured among us without the aid of an institution, in which men of God may have special facilities for improving their minds. And hence we may justly infer the importance, if not the necessity, of the theological school recently opened among us, in which all who are called to the work may find education at their own expense or of the benevolent when they have no private resources.

Having made the foregoing remarks in the hope of correcting the misapprehensions of some and of silencing the cavils of others, we shall now proceed to prove and illustrate the importance of education for ministers of the Gospel.

All must grant that the chief endeavors of a minister should be, first, to understand the Bible himself, and secondly, to teach it to others. On this view then of ministerial duties we ground our proofs, which must accordingly be arranged under two heads.

4. *Ministers need education, because it will greatly assist them in studying and understanding the Scriptures.*

It is often said that the Bible is an easy book; and so doubtless it is in a certain sense. It is easy to be understood as to things most desirable

APPENDIX 1

to be known, for no scholarship is required in order to make out the way of salvation and the principal duties incumbent on man. Yet even the way of life is so intelligible, not because it is always expressed with clearness, but because it is stated so often and in so great a variety of terms, that a person of the commonest apprehension cannot fail, as we may say, to catch the idea. For instance, it is possible that an ignorant man may not comprehend what is meant by "being born again;" yet he will, almost without fail, know what is meant by "repenting" and "believing," which are only different expressions for the saving change intended by regeneration. So also, the declaration that "the blood of Christ cleanseth from all sin,"[283] though quite intelligible to a Jew or any one conversant with the law of Moses, can scarcely suggest the proper idea to an ignorant mind; yet the very truth here taught is elsewhere stated in the plainest manner, as when it is declared that God forgives sin for the sake of Christ. But while it is thankfully admitted, that "he who runs may read"[284] the things which belong to his peace; yet all must allow that there are "some things hard to be understood, which they that are unlearned and unstable wrest to their own destruction"[285]; and many will be ready even to confess that the Bible is a difficult book. And who that knows the history and contents of the sacred volume, can wonder at its difficulties? A collection of writings that are of such high antiquity, several of them being the most ancient in existence, that were composed by Orientals for the use in the first place of people whose mode of living, thinking, and speaking differed widely from our own, that treat on the most sublime and abstruse subjects, and that too in languages which have long since ceased to be spoken, and therefore not easily mastered, and that have been handed down for many generations by the labor of the pen, which is a process far less favorable to correctness than printing—surely a collection of such a character, must be expected to contain parts exceedingly obscure to us, however clear they may have been to the first readers.

---

[283] Cf. 1 John 1:7.
[284] Habbakuk 2:2.
[285] 2 Peter 3:16.

JESUS, WONDROUS SAVIOUR

How then, we ask, can an untaught preacher understand these obscure and seemingly unintelligible portions of the divine oracles? Will commentaries suffice to instruct him? We think not. Some of these may doubtless often help, but they seldom satisfy a person that is intent, as every minister ought to be, on discovering the sense of every part. A sensible and inquisitive reader of a commentary always feels desirous of forming an opinion for himself as to the soundness of the critical remarks and the various attempts at explanation, which abound in such a work; but this he cannot do without possessing a considerable knowledge of the original languages of the Scriptures, not to mention other aids to biblical interpretation. It is a fact that many have been induced to learn Greek and Hebrew in consequence of meeting with some words in these languages in an exposition or critical remark. But while it must be the desire of every intelligent reader to form a deliberate judgment on the sense of Holy Writ, how much more ought every professed and public expounder of the lively oracles both to desire and to be able to form an enlightened and matured opinion. He at least should never be under the necessity of believing implicitly what this or that expositor asserts. He ought to be scholar enough to put to the test the correctness of the criticisms of others, and to discover some of the shades of meaning and valuable hints, which the original words often present but which commentators seldom point out. We have, for example, a word of this kind in Philippians 3:20, where the Greek term πολίτευμα, which is rendered *conversation*, may suggest that heaven is the Christian's country—that his conduct is ruled by heaven's laws—that his desires and affections centre in heaven—and that his permanent abode will finally be in heaven.

We must then maintain, that notwithstanding all the common helps which exist for explaining the Bible, a minister is not likely to gain a competent understanding of its meaning without possessing himself a good degree of learning and information. Can it be expected that an unread person, however good his natural abilities may be, will properly comprehend the prophetical writings? As to unfulfilled prophecies, it is generally admitted that they are often too difficult for even the ablest of interpreters; as was strikingly exemplified in the case of Calvin, who, in his commentaries on the New Testament, omitted the book of Revelation, because he could not, with all his matchless penetration and excellent erudition, discover its meaning. But even predictions that have been accomplished, such as those relating to Babylon, Tyre, and other places in the East, cannot be thoroughly understood and turned to good purpose as evidences of a divine revelation except by one who is conversant with the ancient and modern history of the nations and countries spoken of by the prophet as well as with the original language. Can anyone, for instance, make out a striking and convincing meaning in the promise "to open before Cyrus the two leaved gates,"[286] unless he is aware that such gates were actually left open in Babylon at the time when the city was taken by that conqueror? Also in other parts, in which precepts or doctrines are laid down, obscurities occur, which cannot be readily and satisfactorily removed without a knowledge of Hebrew or Greek. Thus in 1 John 3:3, "every man that hath this hope in him, purifieth himself," the words *in him* are often taken to signify *within himself*, while they in reality mean *on him*, i.e., Christ, as a mere glance at the Greek will show beyond dispute.

5. *Ministers need education because it will enable them more effectually to explain the Scriptures to others.*

When a minister of the Word acquires sacred knowledge, it is not so much that he may enrich himself as that he may dispense it to those who are ignorant and out of the way. "Therefore every scribe, instructed unto the kingdom of heaven, is like to a householder, who bringeth forth out of his treasure things new and old."[287] But to communicate truth to others is often difficult even for some, who find it easy to investigate and discover it for themselves. It is therefore one of the main objects of good literary training to obviate this difficulty by imparting a facility to express whatever useful ideas the mind has acquired. There are two modes of communicating instruction, viz., speaking and writing; and in both these, it is desirable that a religious

---

[286] Isaiah 45:1.
[287] Matthew 13:52.

teacher should be competent to explain and enforce the truths of revelation. The education then for which we plead will teach him how to express in an intelligible, if not attractive form, his own discoveries and views to his hearer or reader. For it will teach him how to define terms and so to distinguish accurately between them. Inability or negligence in this particular is well known to be the cause of much confusion and many hot disputes in theology. Thus, a preacher once maintained that the atonement of Christ is made in heaven for sinners as they repent and consequently scandalized many of his hearers, who believed that it had been already completed on the cross. Now had he stated exactly what he meant by the term "atonement," which was evidently an actual reconciliation to God, none of his hearers could object to his opinion, though they might to his language.

Proper mental discipline will also tend to make a minister observe sequence and method in his remarks, so that his discourses will not present a confused mass of ideas, jumbled together without connection and without design. Good arrangement or method is as necessary in a sermon as sound tactics in the marshalling of an army for battle. What prudent general would ever bring his forces into conflict without order and design? No more should a preacher advance a multitude of remarks that are loose and have no common bearing; for if he be without aim, the hearer must be expected to feel no interest and consequently to receive no instruction. If the ambassador of Christ has no specific message, but speaks altogether at random without having a definite object to accomplish, how can he expect to be heard with attention and respect? Can any minister "excel to the edifying of the church," who does not seek out "acceptable words," and who is not prepared like Paul, "to reason of righteousness, temperance and judgment to come"?[288] All sensible men would scout[289] a public lecturer on any literary or scientific subject, who should talk incoherently, without either sound reasoning or lucid arrangement. But are not coherency and cogency in discourse as much to be expected from a teacher of heavenly truth? Or has he a special

---

[288] 1 Corinthians 14:12; Ecclesiastes 12:10; Acts 24:25.
[289] A rare use of the verb "to scout," meaning "to reject with scorn."

privilege, seeing that his themes are so sacred and momentous, to express his thoughts in a confused and unedifying form? God forbid. Rather as the truths which he has to propound transcend all others in importance, so he ought to excel in clear and convincing discourse. He ought to be able to discuss an article of our holy Faith in a style as methodical and cogent as that in which the great apostle has treated the doctrine of the resurrection in 1 Corinthians 15. Now all these qualifications for public teaching are more or less the results of the intellectual discipline, which must always accompany a good education. There are various branches of study, which directly tend to impart these benefits, especially philology, mathematics, logic, and metaphysics. It is scarcely possible for a person of good understanding to pursue these studies without acquiring a habit of thinking and speaking with clearness and precision, if not with elegance.

With the ability to explain the truths of Scripture is closely allied the power to defend them. A minister should, above all men, "be ready always to give an answer to everyone that asketh a reason of the hope that is in him."[290] But in numerous instances he cannot do this without the aid of education. As learning has often been employed to propagate error, and even to assail the Bible, learning must also be needed to advocate the truth. Who does not see the necessity that a professed teacher of religion should be [a] sufficient scholar to explode the learned criticisms with which many endeavor to bolster up errors? For instance, our distinguishing practice as Baptists often needs a learned advocate; not indeed because a plain reader of the Bible cannot discover his duty, but because there is often a great boast of learning on the other side. There are too many disputants who, as the erudite and candid Dr. G. Campbell remarks, "maintain in defiance of etymology and use, that the word rendered in the New Testament *baptize* means more properly to sprinkle than to plunge, and in defiance of all antiquity, that the former method was the earliest, and, for many centuries, the most general practice in baptizing."[291] Ought not our

---

[290] 1 Peter 3:15.
[291] George Campbell, *Lectures on Pulpit Eloquence* (London: John Bumpus, 1824), 304–305.

ministers then be prepared to expose the ignorance and temerity of such disputants?

Need we advance more in proof of the importance of an educated ministry? Then we would appeal to facts. Have not all the eminent Reformers of the church in every age been learned men? Have not all the ablest expositors and advocates of the truth as it is in Jesus been men of learning? Are the best missionaries ignorant persons, who know neither Greek nor Hebrew? Are not educated ministers in our churches found in general more acceptable, efficient, and successful, than those who neglect and despise literary culture?

Having thus, beloved brethren, laid before you the subject of ministerial education, we cannot close without affectionately urging you to support the theological institution now established among us. Will you permit it to decline and fall by withholding from it your prayers and contributions? Will those who have the means to provide education for pious and gifted young men, who thirst for improvement, deny them any assistance? Unfaithfulness in this matter must be positive treachery to the cause. But, brethren, we hope better things of you. And may the love and mercy of God, through Christ Jesus, be with you all continually and abundantly

Appendix 2

The Statement of Faith in the Toronto Baptist College Act of Incorporation

The Toronto Baptist College Act of Incorporation (December 1, 1880) specified that the College was

> for the education and training of students preparing for and intending to be engaged in pastoral, evangelical, missionary or other denomination work in connection with the Regular Baptist Denomination whereby is intended Regular Baptist Churches exclusively composed of persons who have been baptized on a personal profession of their Faith in Christ holding and maintaining substantially the following doctrines. ... The Divine Inspiration of the Scriptures of the Old and New Testaments and their absolute Supremacy and Sufficiency in matters of faith and practice; the existence of one living and true God, sustaining the personal relation of Father Son and Holy Spirit, the same in essence and equal in attributes, the total and universal depravity of mankind, the election and effectual calling of all God's people, the atoning efficacy of the Death of Christ, the free justification of believers in Him by His imputed Righteousness, the preservation unto eternal life of the Saints, the necessity and efficacy of the influence of the Spirit in regeneration and sanctification, the resurrection of the dead, both just and unjust; the general judgment, the everlasting happiness of the righteous and the everlasting misery of the wicked, immersion in the name of the Father the Son and the Holy Spirit, the only gospel "baptism," that parties so baptized are alone entitled to Communion at the Lord's Table and that a Gospel Church is a Body of baptized believers voluntarily associated for the service of God."[292]

---

[292] Cited G.A. Rawlyk, "A.L. McCrimmon, H.P. Whidden, T.T. Shields, Christian Education, and McMaster University" in his ed., *Canadian Baptists and Christian Higher Education* (Kingston, ON; Montreal, QC: McGill-Queen's University Press, 1988), 33.

Augustus Stephen Vogt, the organist at Jarvis Street Baptist Church

Appendix 3:

Worship at Jarvis Street Baptist Church—a newspaper account from April, 1895[293]

To attend a service at Jarvis Street Baptist Church is to be reminded of the old-fashioned times when people believed in the presence of the Almighty in the temples dedicated to his service. They were good old times. People read with a simple faith how the glory of the Lord descended upon the tabernacle in the wilderness and abode there; and many a bare and barn-like structure has been made a very Holy of Holies by the thought that there, too, the power of the Lord was present to heal. We have got it into our heads now that there is not much we can believe, and we are apologetic rather than hearty about creeds. Still there are places here and there, where the old trust in God and consciousness of his presence seem not only to exist but to flourish. I think Jarvis Street Baptist Church is one of these, and I think, too, that the secret of its vigorous life and the high spirituality of its ideals is to be found in its simple faith and its grasp of that wonderful thought of the divine immanence; partly traditional to Baptists, whose elder divines thought much of the divine majesty and glory, and partly also—may it not be said—the result of immediate irradiation. I do not think anyone possessing even a moderate amount of spiritual insight could attend a service at Jarvis Street Church without feeling that there was something about the place that could be written of in no flippant spirit; an indefinable note of sincere worship, to which all considerations of personal kind, such as the popularity and preaching power of its minister, all musical and architectural features, are merely subsidiary.

Given this central and inspiring fact, everything else follows. The soul clothes itself with a body. So far as the outward characteristics of the church are concerned, it may be said that they are exceedingly satisfactory and attractive. Situated at the corner of Gerrard Street on Jarvis, the Baptist Church is an ornament to the fine thoroughfare on

---

[293] J.R.N., "Pew and Pulpit in Toronto.—VII. At Jarvis Street Baptist Church," *The Week* (April 5. 1895): 438–440.

133

which it stands. Its style may be called auditorium-Gothic, and the corner of its handsome pile is rendered complete by as graceful a tower and spire as there is in Toronto. I have sometimes regretted, when I have looked at it, that the spire is constructed of wood and sheet metal instead of stone, and I have also been rather inclined to criticize the roof, which is weakened in its effect by the necessity of conforming to the circular plan of the auditorium, but let that pass: auditorium-Gothic gives problems to the architect such as never troubled the mediæval men and the man who gets over them at all creditably ought to be complimented rather than found fault with. Mark, when you are passing, the excellence of the stonework, how honest and thorough it is, and the delightful colour and fitness of it. It looks as though the solicitude of the building committee had been extended to each separate stone. The pointing of the joints is a work of conscientious art, and the cut stone work at the doorway and windows is so accurately fitted, piece by piece, that you could not put a ten-cent piece between them. The Jarvis Street Baptist Church is, I believe, the only one in the city that pays municipal taxes, but this evidently does not prevent the greatest attention being paid to its fabric. Indeed, from the look of it, I am inclined to think that if a single stone of it displayed incipient signs of weather-wear a committee meeting would be at once held, and a new stone be substituted without the least delay. The supplemental buildings of the church—Sunday Schools, vestries, etc.—form part of its design as a group, and are very commodious and convenient. Entering the church, you find it spacious and comfortable, quietly and tastefully decorated, and pleasant and restful to the eye. There is an unmistakable home-like feeling about it. It does not subdue you by any mystery of ecclesiasticism, yet no one could have any doubt that it is set apart for a place of worship. The circular idea is carried out both on the lower auditorium and the very capacious gallery. The front of this gallery is of bronzed cast-iron work. Bronzed columns support it, and run up to the junctions of the groined arches of the ceiling that covers it. The central ceiling is circular and flat, with a bold ornamental moulding around it. This and the rest of the roof and the walls is painted—not kalsomined[294]—and the colour and effect of it are very pleasing. The general colour of the woodwork is brown, especially effective in the flat plain masses of the organ front, which is not teased into unnecessary decorations, but rises from the speaker's platform in tall substantial panels, contrasting with the well-chosen yellowish drabs of the walls and ceiling. This brown woodwork is very effective. Care has also been taken in the gilding and ornamentation of the organ pipes which are not too glaring or effusively aureotint.[295] The floor of the church is covered throughout with a carpet which is mainly crimson, and there are crimson cushions in all the seats; the result of all that I have mentioned being an interior of great comfort—a place that it would be pleasant to sit and read in even if there were no other attractions but those of subdued light, well-chosen colour, an atmosphere of gentle warmth. Seated thus, we will say in the gallery, one sees that the speaker's platform, which is immediately in front of the organ, is a lengthened oblong. There is a recess in the organ front which is occupied by an open baptistery of white marble, accessible by concealed steps at either end. At either end of the recess and placed close to the organ front is a massive gothic chair of oak with red cushions, and midway between them is a brass lectern, at which the minister stands to preach. There is no pulpit. In front of the speaker's platform are the choir-pews, facing the auditorium and arranged in curves. Beyond these, again, and separated from the auditorium by a panelled division is the keyboard of the organ and the organist's seat. It will be understood, therefore, that when Dr. Thomas preaches, he preaches, literally though not metaphorically, "over the heads" of the choir and organist.

In the old-fashioned ways of thinking in vogue at the Jarvis Street Baptist Church, however, the people who attend it are more important than the architecture, or the decoration, or the shape of the organ front; and if their thought were put into words it would perhaps be that they care more to be themselves, "lively stones," "polished after the similitude of a palace," than to have the best of material edifices.

---

[294] I.e., whitewashed.
[295] I.e., tinted with gold.

JESUS, WONDROUS SAVIOUR

They begin to crowd into the church in great numbers towards eleven o'clock, and by the time the hour of service arrives the lower auditorium, which will hold about 800 or 900 people, is comfortably full.

On the occasion of my visit there were perhaps a hundred people in the gallery at the morning service. It was a representative Toronto audience of the best class. There were many families there; the heads, solid, intelligent, serious-looking men of business, the result of whose sober, righteous, and godly lives was visible in their faces; their wives, women who had something besides fashion and frivolity to think of; their children, the carefully-nurtured offspring of prayer and good example. The proportion of men in the congregation is large, and their general type seemed to be one of intelligence and high character. While the congregation was assembling, the organist, Mr. A.S. Vogt,[296] came in and took his seat at the organ key-board. The choir soon followed. It was composed of sixteen women choristers, and ten or twelve men. Precisely at eleven o'clock the pastor, Rev. B.D. Thomas, D.D., came in and took his seat in one of the large chairs. He is a portly man; looks in robust health and his head is massive and striking; his face very genial and intelligent, and his eyes have a glance that little children would not be afraid of. He has simple and unaffected dignity but is not pompous. On the contrary there is a reality and naturalness about all he does that are very charming. He has the humility that comes from the contemplation of great things, and I should think his people find that he has a good deal of sunshine in his nature. His hair—there is a good deal of it—is passing from iron-gray to white, but he reads without glasses and his florid colour tells of great vitality. He is robust, but you soon know that he is a man of delicate taste and gentle feeling. You might go far and not meet with such a wholesome, sane, kindly-human yet high-souled prophet. For I came to the conclusion before

---

[296] Augustus Stephen Vogt (1861–1926) is remembered as the founder of the Toronto Mendelssohn Choir and from 1918 till his death the Dean of the Faculty of Music at the University of Toronto. See Barclay McMillan, Elaine Keillor, Ruth Pincoe, and Andrew Mcintosh, "Augustus Vogt," *The Canadian Encyclopedia* (https://www.thecanadianencyclopedia.ca/en/article/augustus-stephen-vogt; accessed June 8, 2023).

APPENDIX 3

the service was over that Dr. Thomas was a prophet, and that if he preached in a shed instead of Jarvis Street Church, he would soon have a prophet's congregation. I don't call him an orator—oratory and the prophetic gift are different things. What I mean to say is that he has a message; where it comes from I will not pretend to say, but as long as he speaks you are bound to listen to him and you never wish that he would cut his message short. Add to these things a pleasant, not over strong voice, a rather rapid utterance, and a hearty and genuine manner, and you have some idea of Dr. Thomas. He seems too much taken up with his work to have any thought of himself, and he is not one of those mannerists who, in dispensing the Water of Life, cannot help putting into it a tincture of their own personality.

How does this warm-hearted, good, sympathetic man approach the problems of human life? Broadly speaking, with an implicit faith in God and a realization of his power and goodness and presence in the world that are strong enough to overcome all doubt and darkness. You gather as you listen to his earnest prayers and to his preaching that he holds that while God cannot be known and searched out by the human intellect, he may be apprehended by a spiritual insight, and that he is ready to come by his Spirit into the hearts of all. That in Adam we all died; that in Christ we may all be made alive. That Adam, made in perfection, fell, and that since his fall there is no way of salvation for man along the road of endeavour to obey the moral law. "All the bridges on that road are broken down and to attempt to walk in it would be spiritually suicidal." That we are not to govern ourselves by our sentimental conceptions of what the government of the world ought to be, but by the revelation of God's method of salvation as shown in his Word. That Christ made on Calvary a sacrifice of infinite virtue, and that believing on him, and trusting in that sacrifice, we shall be saved. That all who are in Christ will "crucify the flesh with its affections and lusts," and will "walk in the Spirit." That "Christ is able to save unto the uttermost all who come unto God by him," and that there is "no other way." That these things present difficulties to the human intellect which are to be surmounted only by faith. In fact, to listen to Dr. Thomas is to be reminded of the orthodoxy of thirty or forty years ago; before "the higher criticism" was thought of or Darwin had written. He would say, I take it, that the problems of religion transcend human reason and cannot be successfully approached by science.

The service was begun by the whole congregation rising and singing heartily, "Praise God from whom all blessings flow," to the Old Hundredth.[297] Then the pastor led in prayer, after which a hymn was sung of a simple old-fashioned kind, but musical enough to show that the choir was well chosen and admirably balanced, both men's and women's voices being above the ordinary in quality. Then Dr. Thomas read in a very interesting way the story of the man, in St. John's Gospel, who was blind from his birth. A short chant, a reading from the book of Job, a longer prayer, the taking up of the offertory, and another hymn, made up the rest of the preliminary service. The sermon was based upon the Gospel which had been previously read, and the text was, "Master, who did sin, this man or his parents, that he was born blind. Jesus said: Neither did this man sin nor his parents, but that the works of God might be manifested in him." Beginning with a sympathetic allusion to human suffering, the preacher said that there were instances in which the causes of weakness, crippled limbs, blindness and imbecility could be directly traced to human agency. There were others which were a great mystery. There did not seem to be any adequate reason for them, and it was difficult sometimes to reconcile them with the existence of a merciful Father of the race. We might rest assured, however, that when all accounts were squared—as squared they would be—it would be found that the divine management of the world would be justified. There were some things that we could see now. The existence of such afflicted ones tended to make the rest of us thankful for our mercies. A great honour was thus put upon these who in their measure were sacrifices for us. Had we begun to realize the glory there was in the idea of suffering for others? There was that in it which was calculated to ennoble and transfigure what otherwise seemed dark and perplexing. By our weakness, by our

---

[297] The Old Hundredth is a hymn tune in long metre, from the second edition of the Genevan Psalter and was composed in 1551.

pain, by our sorrow, others might be ministered unto. Through our tears others might smile, by our stripes others might be healed. It seemed that his idea of sacrifice ran through all nature. It might be that even this sin-stricken world had its mission to other planets conceivably inhabited by unfallen intelligences to whom the story of our tears and struggles through the incoming of sin might be known. This is, of course, only the most meagre indication, scarcely an outline, of what Dr. Thomas said. It was a very impressive discourse, with an uplift and inspiration in it for which one could not help being grateful.

The ordinance of the Lord's Supper is observed every Sunday morning at Jarvis Street Church, except on the first Sunday of the month when it is celebrated in the evening. It takes the simplest form. There is a table at the back of the organ key-board on which the bread and wine are placed and covered with a white linen cloth. The deacons carry the elements to the communicants as they sit in the pews; a goodly number of them. Hymn and prayer, a few words from the pastor, and a time for silence, have their part in this feast of remembrance of the Saviour of the world.

The service in the evening differed from that in the morning, only by the addition of two anthems. They were very beautifully sung. I have heard no more finished vocalism in Toronto. People held their breath and sighed when the last tone died away. It differed also from the fact that Dr. Thomas did not read his sermon from manuscript. He did this in the morning, but with such freedom that it could scarcely be told that it was not an extempore discourse. In the evening he preached what he characterized as a "simple gospel sermon, which he trusted he should make so plain that no child there need fail to understand it." He had been preaching that afternoon to a strange but attentive audience of 300 men at the Central Prison.[298] He said that, in a manner, the gospel that was suited to those prisoners was just as suitable to his congregation at the church. His text was, "He is able to save to the uttermost all that come unto God by him." After the

---

[298] The Central Prison was technically Toronto Central Prison. It was located at the intersection of King Street and Strachan Avenue. It opened in 1873 and was closed in 1915. It was demolished five years later.

service, the ordinance of believer's baptism was administered to two young men. While a hymn was being sung the pastor retired, and in a short time appeared in the baptistery, clothed in a black gown. The candidates then came one after another from the concealed steps and were gently plunged backward beneath the water by Dr. Thomas, who said, "Upon a profession of thy faith in Christ, I baptize thee in the name of the Father, the Son and the Holy Ghost; Amen." He also spoke to them before their baptism encouraging and hopeful words, and said that he prayed that "from that burial with Christ in baptism they would rise to newness of life." Then, speaking from the water, his hand on the marble edge of the baptistery, the pastor addressed a few words on the ordinance of baptism to the congregation. He said that Baptists did not attribute any sacramental efficacy to the water of baptism. They considered they were simply following the command of Christ as laid down in the New Testament. Let them examine that volume for themselves, which was joined in with deep attention by the vast congregation from beginning to end.

www.ingramcontent.com/pod-product-compliance
Lightning Source LLC
Chambersburg PA
CBHW071510040426
42444CB00008B/1572